D1273711

The Team Leader's Idea-a-Day Guide

250 Ways to Make Your Team More Effective and Productive — Every Working Day of the Year

Susan Fowler Woodring

Drea Zigarmi, Ph.D.

DARTNELL

4660 N RAVENSWOOD AVE, CHICAGO, IL 60640-4595 PHONE: (800) 621-5463

Dartnell is a publisher serving the world of business with books, manuals, newsletters and bulletins, and training materials for executives, managers, supervisors, salespeople, financial officials, personnel executives, and office employees. Dartnell also produces management and sales training videos and audiocassettes, publishes many useful business forms, and many of its materials and films are available in languages other than English. Dartnell, established in 1917, serves the world's business community. For details, catalogs, and product information, write:

THE DARTNELL CORPORATION

4660 N Ravenswood Ave
Chicago, IL 60640-4595, U.S.A.
or phone (800) 621-5463 in U.S. and Canada

This publication is designed to provide accurate and authoritative information in regard to the subject matter covered. It is sold with the understanding that the publisher is not engaged in rendering legal, accounting, or other professional service. If legal advice or other expert assistance is required, the services of a competent professional person should be sought.

— *From a Declaration of Principles jointly adopted by a Committee of the American Bar Association and a Committee of Publishers.*

Copyright 1997 in the United States, Canada, and Britain by
THE DARTNELL CORPORATION
Library of Congress Catalog Card Number: 97-67276
ISBN 0-85013-295-9

Printed in the United States

ACKNOWLEDGMENTS

The co-authors would like to thank Vera Derr at Dartnell for the opportunity of writing this book and Angela Yokoe for helping pull it together; Rick Schaffer and Diane LaChapelle, who pitched in when E-mail failed; Kelie Schilenger and Tammy Williams, who helped us communicate when international boundaries made it difficult; Kip Woodring, the greatest "silent co-author" who ever existed; and a special nod to our friends, colleagues, and clients at Blanchard Training and Development for our many years of learning together that ultimately made this book possible.

DEDICATION

To Lisa and Alexa, who will need to use these ideas in the next century, and to Mother Earth, whose essential nature is a constant source of growth for me.

— Drea Zigarmi

To Nancy, Mark, and Sharon and our "Happy Team," who unwittingly became the laboratory for testing these ideas and the very nature of teams. It is through you that I've learned much about myself.

— Susan Fowler Woodring

ABOUT THE AUTHORS

DR. DREA ZIGARMI, PhD

Drea Zigarmi is the president of Zigarmi Associates, Inc., and the director of research and development for Blanchard Training and Development, Inc. His work has been critical to the success of Situational Leadership II, one of the most widely used research-based management models in the world. Dr. Zigarmi has co-authored with Ken Blanchard and Pat Zigarmi the best selling book, *Leadership and the One Minute Manager*. He and Dr. Blanchard are also co-authors of the well-known "Leader Behavior Analysis" (LBA) instrument and two new instruments, the "Leader Action Profile" (LAP) and "Team Member Action Profile" (T-MAP). Drea developed the DISCovering Self and Others training program with Dr. Michael O'Connor to teach people how to understand behavioral patterns.

Dr. Zigarmi is recognized worldwide as an expert on leadership and a teacher for such clients as Aerospace, Honda, Siemans Medical, the Marmaxx Group, and a number of professional sports franchises. His 15 years as a consultant have helped produce significant bottom-line results and the adoption of management-development programs, performance-appraisal systems, and productivity-improvement projects built around the concepts of Situational Leadership II.

Zigarmi received his B.A. in science from Norwich University and a master's in philosophy and doctorate in administration and organizational behavior from the University of Massachusetts in Amherst.

Drea Zigarmi can be contacted at Zigarmi and Associates, Inc. in Escondido, California (619) 489-5005.

SUSAN FOWLER WOODRING

Recognized as a witty, warm, and captivating speaker, Susan Fowler Woodring has presented her seminars and workshops on leadership from a self, one-on-one, and team perspective, in all 50 states and 19 foreign countries. While she is grateful for her success and loves the opportunity to impact audiences from the platform, she is equally immersed in her role as author and budding researcher. Susan believes that ultimately it will be the quality of her message, not just the polished delivery, that will spark the insights and stimulate people to make changes for themselves and their organization.

Susan is co-author with Dr. Ken Blanchard and Dr. Laurence Hawkins of the Situational Self Leadership training program being adopted for thousands of employees worldwide by companies such as Dow Corning, Caterpillar, TJ Maxx, Marshalls, Home Savings of America, Nokia, and Pepsico. She is also co-author of several instruments including the Developmental Needs Analysis (DNA) with Dr. Drea Zigarmi and the Empowerment Development Gauge and Evaluation (EDGE).

For more information regarding seminars, speeches or consulting, contact Susan Fowler Woodring at Blanchard Training and Development, (800) 728-6000; online: susanw@ blanchardtraining.com; fax: (619) 233-5340.

INTRODUCTION

One of the beautiful aspects of native American cultures is the integrated relationship of the individual to nature and society. Did you know that in the Hopi language, for instance, there is only one noun — "it." We might say, "The table is brown." The Hopi would say, "It tables brownly." They see themselves as connected to all things, and their language allows them to maintain that connection.

To become a High Impact Team, or HIT, and remain one over time, members must see themselves as connected to each other. There is no "I" in team. What is done to one is done to self. We might say, "You and I belong to the same team." The Hopi would say, "It teams."

How do cultures, like most modern western cultures, develop an appreciation and ability to team when the very strength of these societies came from the rugged individualist? The 250 Ideas in *The Team Leader's Idea-A-Day Guide* are a start. Teams must have the Hopi ideal of connectedness, while recognizing the importance and contribution of individuals. After all, it is the very differences of team members that make the team powerful.

This book has two components, *Ideas* and *Worksheets* — one for each day of the year. Together they provide the direction and support you need to help establish the team's vision and values, tasks and norms that will create a oneness of passion and creative productivity. *Ideas* are key concepts, important insights, facts, and step-by-step processes you need in order to start, develop, and sustain your team. *Worksheets* guide you through the chartering process, assess team member's perceptions, and help organize yourself and your team to peak performance.

The Team Leader's Idea-A-Day Guide is organized into three sections that relate to the life of your team:

> Section One — Beginning Ideas: Setting Teams Up to Win
>
> Section Two — Developing Ideas: Helping Teams Operate More Effectively
>
> Section Three — Sustaining Ideas: Rejuvenating or Ending a Team's Work

- You can choose to begin at the beginning and work your way through the ideas from starting your team to ending the team with honorable closure; or
- Select a section and chapter devoted to a particular team issue or topic; or
- Flip through the book and single out an idea that makes sense today.

If you choose to begin at the beginning, the Ideas and Worksheets in each section will guide you through a Team Game Plan:

Step 1

- Determine why you need a team.

Step 2

- Understand the characteristics of a team vs. a High Impact Team (HIT).

Step 3

- Select the type of team you need.

Step 4

- Identify the team sponsor (who is not the team leader), and/or
- Identify the team leader (who is not the sponsor).

Step 5

- Team leader and sponsor initiate the team charter, clearly stating team's purpose, goals, and guidelines.

Step 6

- Decide the size of your team and recruit and select team members.

Step 7

- Plan for creating an effective physical environment and a positive emotional atmosphere.

Step 8

- Bring members together.

Step 9

- Beginning with the purpose and outcomes initially drafted by the sponsor and team leader, the team creates a charter including a statement of purpose, measurable goals, and guidelines to govern the way the team operates.

Step 10

- The team develops processes around meeting structure, problem solving, decision making, conflict resolution, communication, feedback, and rewards and recognition.

Step 11

- Processes and perceptions are assessed, evaluated, and discussed continually.

Step 12

- Consideration is given to emerging leadership, team training, and behavior patterns.

Step 13

- Leadership provides what the team needs at each of the five phases of team evolution.

Step 14

- When the time is right, the team experiences honorable closure and moves on.

If your team is already up and running, but you haven't completed most of the steps in the Team Game Plan, then consider the following approach:

1. First, get a sponsor who is not the team leader, or a team leader who is not a sponsor.
2. Together get agreement on why the team needs to exist; confirm that it is a group with HIT potential; determine the type of team needed; and craft a draft of the charter's purpose and outcomes.
3. Referring to Ideas 5.1–5.15, "Initiating the Charter," and Ideas 8.1–8.28, "Creating the Charter," create the charter with the team.

Then, using the appropriate checklists in Ideas 17.1–17.15, "Assessing Team Process," assess areas that need revamping, issues that need attention, or skills that need improvement.

Building a High Impact Team may be one of the most difficult things you will ever do as a leader, but it will also be among the most rewarding. Think about the experiences you have had as a successful team member in sports, music, dance, church, social club, or work. Remember the energy, the sense of camaraderie, the thrill of success? Now recall the teams that struggled and fell apart and the sense of frustration, perhaps even anger, at the wasted time and opportunity. As a team leader you can make the difference between the best or worst experiences for your team members. It may not be easy, but with *The Team Leader's Idea-A-Day Guide*, it will be much simpler.

TABLE OF CONTENTS

THE TEAM LEADER'S IDEA-A-DAY GUIDE

SECTION 1

BEGINNING IDEAS:
SETTING TEAMS UP TO WIN

Teams are not a passing fad. They are essential to compete in today's dynamic, global workplace. But, most organizations have been frustrated at their attempts to move to more effective teamwork. Why? Because teams don't just happen. They are expensive. They take preparation. They take patience and work. They take talent and skill to make happen.

Teams are not formed just for the sake of having teams, or even to "humanize" the workplace. They are established because the output needed cannot be done by one person.

A team is 4–12 people* who are deeply committed to a clearly stated purpose and who hold themselves, their teammates, and the team accountable for the team's overall result. The difference in a High Impact Team (HIT) is that this commitment to a clearly stated purpose and mutual accountability results in outstanding product or output.

Being a team leader is a sobering responsibility. Despite the collaborative nature of teams, or perhaps because of it, strong leadership is essential.

This section gives you, the team leader or potential team leader, a plan with critical considerations and specific steps to take as you begin creating HITs.

---

*Teams need not be limited to 4–12 people. It is possible to have teams with greater numbers, but usually working units are broken down into smaller performance teams. See Ideas 6.1–6.11, "Optimal Team Size and Selection of Team Members."

IF IT'S TOO LATE FOR BEFORE THOUGHTS:

Go directly to jail. Do not pass go. Do not collect $200.

While in your self-imposed exile, do the following:

1. First, get a sponsor who is not the team leader, or a team leader who is not a sponsor.
2. Together get agreement on why the team needs to exist; confirm that it is a group with HIT potential; determine the type of team needed, and craft a draft of the charter's purpose and outcomes.
3. Create the charter with the team, based on Ideas 5.1–5.15, "Initiating the Charter," and Ideas 8.1–8.28, "Creating the Charter."
4. Then, using the appropriate checklists in Ideas 17.1–17.15, "Assessing Team Process," assess areas that need revamping, issues that need attention, or skills that need improvement.

CHAPTER ONE

WHY TEAMS? WHY NOW?

WHAT'S IN IT FOR YOU?

- Increase support for your team by understanding why organizations need teams
- Enhance chances of attracting good team members by overcoming resistance to teams
- Discover how to appeal to potential team members through benefits of team membership
- Determine if teams are required in your situation

Taking on a team is a big commitment on the team leader's part. In this chapter you will learn why the effort is worth it and how to rally support right from the start.

IDEA

WHAT'S IN IT FOR YOU?

• **Reinforce your organization's need for teams**

WHY TEAMS? WHY NOW?

1.1 Six Cultural and Business Trends Fostering the Use of Teams

As a team leader you need to be aware of the forces promoting a team culture. Evaluate these market trends and determine which ones are pushing your organization toward teams.

1. **Quality customer service.** The tremendous emphasis on building a closer relationship with the customer necessitates quality, speed, and sensitivity to customer demands. This kind of customer service must be done through a seamless set of activities by more than one person.
2. **Increased span of control.** Downsizing has left frontline people with more responsibilities and very little coaching. Teaming is a way to increase the resources for coaching.
3. **Technology and information.** In the era of sophisticated specialization, cross-field, cross-functional collaboration is a must for solving complex problems. The cross-fertilization of ideas and information will happen in teams.
4. **Cultural preference.** Three-fifths of the world population values a collective approach to living and working. The cultures of Africa, Asia, the Middle East, and Latin America show a strong preference for loyalty to a group, tribe, or family. With the globalization of organizations, the need to work in teams has increased.
5. **Sophisticated workforce.** Workers today are more highly educated, come from affluent backgrounds, and expect involvement. They want participation, autonomy, and responsibility, which can most readily be fostered in a team setting.
6. **Unions.** There is a growing emphasis by unions to advocate the adoption of employee involvement systems in order for U.S. companies to become more competitive (Bluestone and Bluestone, 1990).

If your own belief in the team concept begins to flag, remember that in the big picture, teams are coming one way or the other, and sooner rather than later.

I D E A

WHY TEAMS? WHY NOW?

1.2 Eight Ways Your Organization Will Benefit from Teams

If your organization is still trying to determine if teams are worth it, consider the following:

1. **Team output usually exceeds individual output.** While a single person can make a big difference in an organization, he or she rarely has the knowledge, experience, or skill equal to a team. Research is clear that major gains on quality and productivity most often result from organizations with a team culture (Katzenback and Smith, 1993).

2. **Complex problems can be solved more effectively.** Complex problems usually require diverse, in-depth technical knowledge that can be found only among several subject-matter experts. Complexity mandates teams.

3. **Creative ideas are usually stimulated in the presence of other individuals who have the same focus, passion, and excitement.** Creative ideas, or leaps from conventional wisdom, are usually spawned in the tension of differences. This can most easily occur in teams.

4. **Support arises among team members.** Process improvement and product innovation are hard work and take a long time. It would be natural for one person's energy to drop during the long effort. The synergy and optimism that come from people working together productively can sustain team member enthusiasm and support even through difficult times.

5. **Teams infuse knowledge.** When many people work on an organizational problem, more organization members will see the need for change and a vision of what is better. Team members become "sensors" for how the rest of the organization will view the proposed change, as well as ambassadors for the proposed change.

6. **Teams promote organizational learning in a work setting.** The team setting naturally promotes both formal (training events and educational experiences) and informal learning because of the diverse knowledge and skills present in the group members which then are ingested through problem identification and problem solving.

7. **Teams promote individual self-disclosure and examination.** Teams require flexibility in behavior and outlook from individual team members. Egos must be checked at the door in favor of passionate commitment to a common goal.

8. **Teams both appreciate and take advantage of diversity.** Preconceived ideas about people and things will ultimately be challenged in HITs. Emotions and ideas that do not support tolerance will be challenged in HITs.

I D E A

- **Recognize the biggest organizational barriers to teams**

WHY TEAMS? WHY NOW?

1.3 Five Major Reasons Why Organizations Don't Support Teams

There are some very real reasons that HITs are not embraced in an organization. As a team leader you will want to be prepared to overcome organizational bias against teams.

What obstacles do you foresee coming from your organization that will make it difficult to create HITs? Consider the following:

1. **The cost of teams.*** Research has clearly shown that teams are expensive. They cost dollars in the form of time spent by people to complete the team outcomes, hours taken from "regular work," resources required for team operation, and budget requirements to implement team solutions. These costs can be woefully underestimated in the case of teams that are ill-conceived, ill-trained, and poorly monitored.
2. **The rarity of HITs.** Because HITs are rare, it is difficult for top managers to stay focused and sustain the dedication necessary to foster teams in the long run.
3. **Lack of role modeling.** If leaders at the top of the organization don't model team behavior, teams are more difficult to sell throughout the organization. Executives often have false assumptions about how teams can work and what it takes to support a team culture. Heavy time demands, "turfdoms," and the almost innate individualism of top executives result in poor teaming at the top. In fact, many top executives find it difficult to support the concept of teams because they fear the depletion of power that may come with teams.
4. **Poor training.** Team members must be taught the fundamental processes and norms for good team member behavior. Typically, team training is focused on *what* the team is going to do, not *how* it is going to do it. But, even if team process training is done, it must be reinforced to ensure against inflated egos, turf battles, and group disillusionment.
5. **Weak performance standards.** An organization that has weak performance standards will likely not hold teams accountable for determining a clear purpose, sound team processes, or measurable results. An organization with a strong performance focus and ethic, where people are held accountable for performance, creates the soil in which HITs can grow. When organizations with a weak, inconsistent performance emphasis approach teams as an answer to their output problems, teams will be harder to foster.

---

* See "Meeting Structure," Idea 9.4, "The Cost of a Meeting."

I D E A

WHAT'S IN IT FOR YOU?

• **Prepare for resistance from potential team members**

WHY TEAMS? WHY NOW?

1.4 Ten Reported Reasons Why People Resist Team Membership

You will hear them sooner or later — the excuses for not wanting to join a team. Which ones sound familiar? You may find yourself "selling" the team concept to potential team members in the initial phases of team building. Which of the following objections would you have the most difficulty overcoming?

1. Lack of faith that teams really do perform better than individuals.
2. Negative team experiences in the past.
3. Teams take time to develop and do their work, which may not fit the individual's need for work closure.
4. Failure of the company to alter its incentive-compensation practices to include team performance and behaviors.
5. Too much politicking and backroom dealing is done.
6. Personal discomfort and risk inherent in feedback.
7. Teams may slow down individual performance, visibility, and promotions.
8. People like competition and want to take responsibility for their own accomplishments and failures.
9. Teams formed for the sake of job enhancement, communication, or morale seldom become teams and aren't compelling enough to overcome individual reservations.
10. Lack of clear outcomes and worthy purpose.

To diffuse these issues and help your potential team members embrace teams, consider the benefits listed in the next idea.

I D E A

• **Learn benefits that will entice potential team members**

WHY TEAMS? WHY NOW?

1.5 Ten Reported Reasons Why People Want to Be Part of a Team

Whom can you remind today that the "team thing" is a good deal?

1. It's possible to feel more joy when that joy is reflected in the face of another.
2. It's more stimulating to have ideas from other people.
3. No one is smarter than all of us.
4. It is more meaningful to accomplish more with people who are dedicated to the same thing.
5. It is possible to learn more and faster when teaming with people who are as talented as or more talented than the individual.
6. A team member is not alone when facing a problem or feeling discouraged. He or she can get help from other members.
7. Successes are celebrated among the people who understand the meaning of the success.
8. Opportunities exist for understanding the constraints, problems, and benefits that one individual's actions create for others.
9. Team members gain a broader picture of how the organization works or doesn't work by solving problems with others.
10. There is a sense of contributing to something larger than the individual when working as a team.

W O R K S H E E T

WHAT'S IN IT FOR YOU?

• Discover what will motivate a person to join a team

WHY TEAMS? WHY NOW?

1.6 Team Benefits Checklist

Identify potential team members and ask them to rank the following benefits in order of importance to them. Their responses can give you (and them) valuable insights into what will motivate them to embrace teams.

Rank order the following team benefits in the order of their importance to you.

1 = most important
10 = least important

_____ I feel more joy when that joy is reflected in the face of another.

_____ It's more stimulating to have ideas from other people.

_____ No one is smarter than all of us.

_____ It has more meaning to me when I can accomplish more with people who are dedicated to the same thing I am.

_____ I can learn more and faster when I team with people who are as talented as or more talented than I am.

_____ I am not alone when I face a problem or get discouraged. I can get help from others.

_____ I get to celebrate the successes with other people who share my understanding of the meaning of the success.

_____ I have the opportunity to understand the constraints, problems, and benefits that my actions create for others.

_____ I get a broader picture of how the organization works or doesn't work when I problem solve with others.

_____ I get the sense that I am contributing to something larger than myself when I work in a team.

WORKSHEET

- **Determine if your situation requires a team approach**

WHY TEAMS? WHY NOW?

1.7 The "When Are Teams Required?" Checklist

Workloads increase while workforces shrink, but the work issues grow in size, scope, and complexity. People are responsible for day-to-day decisions that have implications far beyond their job at the moment. Teams may seem an obvious antidote.

But, in order for teams to be truly effective and worth the effort, certain conditions should exist. If you answer "yes" to four of the seven questions below, a team is essential.

	Yes	No
1. Is the situation or problem too complex for any one person to understand or solve?	❏	❏
2. Is the outcome interdependent on the activities of several individuals?	❏	❏
3. Are communication and connectivity essential to the overall success of the outcome?	❏	❏
4. Does a viable solution depend on mutual problem solving?	❏	❏
5. Is the expertise required for successful performance spread among several key individuals?	❏	❏
6. Is the decision-making process essential for people's commitment to implement the solution?	❏	❏
7. Is there a specific performance challenge that is so clear and passionate that it will serve as the greatest motivator?	❏	❏

CHAPTER TWO

WHAT IS A HIGH IMPACT TEAM?

WHAT'S IN IT FOR YOU?

- Determine if you are the leader of a group and a team
- Learn the difference between a team leader, sponsor, and member
- Find out if your team has the characteristics of a High Impact Team (HIT)

Although the terms are often used interchangeably, there is a difference between a group and a team. In this chapter you will learn to distinguish between the two and why it makes such a difference in your role as a team leader.

I D E A

WHAT IS A HIGH IMPACT TEAM?

2.1 The Difference Between Groups and Teams

According to the dictionary, the difference between a group and a team is that a *group* is simply a collection of people that may be related in some way; a *team* is a number of people associated in a joint action. In other words, a team is a group of people who are expected to do something together. It is important to understand this distinction because the two entities require very different things over the course of time. As a leader, you, too, will have very different things required of you.

So, just because you're responsible for a group of people does not make them a team or you a team leader. What does? The two most important distinctions are:

1. **Interdependence.** If one person's performance depends on the performance of another, the two are interdependent. It takes hard work and willingness for individuals to put aside the "disease of me" as Pat Riley* calls it, and strive for true interdependence with others.

2. **Potential for self-leadership.** Ironically, the only way a group can become a team is through strong leadership, and the only way a team can become a HIT is if that leader is willing — when the time is right — to let go and let the team members take on the responsibilities of leading themselves.

The Group or Team Comparison grid on the next page provides additional comparisons be-tween a group and a team.

Working Group	Team
A number of people who work together and make decisions to further their own or departmental goals	A number of people who convene, work, and decide together because of their passion for a common vision and outcomes
Specific people are responsible for the effectiveness of the group.	All members see the effectiveness of the group as their responsibility.
Individual issues take precedence.	Individual issues are subservient to team issues.
People are skeptical of cross-functional relationships because they fear a reduction of individual or departmental power.	People you lead want and create cross-functional relationships.
They see challenges on an individual basis.	People you lead see challenges as a group issue.
The group is not as important as the issues.	The team and the work the team is doing are equally important and enjoyable.
Interdependence should be kept to a minimum because it breeds dependence.	Interdependence is high.
Individuals judge their own performance in relation to the group.	The individual sees own success or failure in terms of the group's success or failure.
Interpersonal and team skills are not valued or discussed.	Lack of interpersonal skills is pointed out through open feedback and discussed.
Collaboration and synergy are infrequent and not seen as necessary for success.	Collaboration and synergy are typical.

*Pat Riley, *The Winner Within: A Life Plan for Team Players* (New York: Berkeley Publishing Group, 1993).

WORKSHEET

WHAT'S IN IT FOR YOU?

• **Practice distinguishing between a group and a team**

WHAT IS A HIGH IMPACT TEAM?

2.2 Is It a Group or Is It a Team?

Before you evaluate whether you're leading a group or a team, practice on the examples below. Use the Group or Team Comparison grid in Idea 2.1 to determine which of the following groups of people are a team. Place a checkmark beside the groups that you believe qualify as teams.

- Sales reps for a manufacturer who come together to gain product knowledge and learn sales techniques
- The Atlanta Braves Baseball Club
- The U.S. Women's Gymnastics Team
- The White House Staff
- Nightshift piece workers
- Employees brought together to create the organization's mission statement

Answers:

- The sales reps are a group because there is no interdependence. As a group, their purpose and goals are individual rather than collective.
- The Atlanta Braves are a team because the members have a common purpose, goals, and outcomes.
- The U.S. Women's Gymnastics squad is a group when each woman is vying for an individual title. They come together as a team when vying for the team medal and each performance contributes to team points.
- The White House Staff is a team, interdependent with an appointed leader, assigned roles and responsibilities, and a common purpose and goals.
- The nightshift workers are a group unless they are working together on a special task force or they are structured so that each person's job influences the performance of another's.
- The group creating the mission statement is a team because — aha! — they have a common mission.

W O R K S H E E T

WHAT'S IN IT FOR YOU?

• Determine if you're leading a group or a team

WHAT IS A HIGH IMPACT TEAM?

2.3 Are You a Group Leader or a Team Leader?

To get a sense of whether you're dealing with a group or a team, circle the numbers of the descriptions that fit you, your team, and the team members.

1	The people you lead work together and make decisions to further their own or departmental goals.	9	The people you lead see their success or failure in terms of group success or failure.
2	The people you lead convene, work, and decide together because of their passion for a common vision and outcomes.	10	You are responsible for the effectiveness of the group over time.
3	Individual issues take precedence.	11	The people you lead see the effectiveness of the group as their responsibility.
4	The people you lead are skeptical of cross-functional relationships because they fear a reduction of individual or departmental power.	12	The people you lead see challenges on an individual basis.
5	Individual issues are subservient to team issues.	13	The people you lead want and create cross-functional relationships.
6	The people you lead want interdependence to be high.	14	The people you lead feel interdependence should be kept to a minimum because it breeds dependence.
7	The people you lead see challenges as a group issue.	15	Collaboration and synergy are infrequent and are not seen as necessary for success.
8	The people you lead judge their own performance in relation to the group.	16	Collaboration and synergy are typical.

Answers:

Team Responses: 2, 5, 6, 7, 9, 11, 13, 16

Group Responses: 1, 3, 4, 8, 10, 12, 14, 15

If you chose six or more Team Responses, there's a high probability that you and your group of people consider yourselves a team and are working toward becoming a HIT. If you had six or more Group Responses, then you will need to start from the beginning to build a foundation for teamwork.

I D E A

WHAT'S IN IT FOR YOU?

- Clarify the primary roles necessary for creating HITs

WHAT IS A HIGH IMPACT TEAM?

2.4 Role Call

While these roles may vary across teams and organizations, they need to be considered for the success of your team:

TEAM SPONSOR

Every team should have a sponsor — whether it is an individual or another group or agency. For example: the Warren Commission sponsored by the Justice Department, the reorganization team sponsored by the organization's Board of Directors.

A team sponsor authorizes and defines the boundaries of the team. The sponsor can also be the liaison between the team and the rest of the organization. The team will benefit if the sponsor is *not* an active member of the team. This may be difficult, but worth it.* The sponsor's role is to clarify the team's purpose and provide the team the resources and advice it needs to be effective.

The sponsor should define the connection between the team and the organization. The sponsor is a conduit for assistance and information for the team. The sponsor may also be an ally, an advocate, or a political advisor to the team.

DESIGNATED TEAM LEADER

While eventually HITs will have shared leadership, a designated team leader is needed in the initial stages of a team's inception. A leader is usually appointed by the organization and is directly responsible and accountable for team results. The leader may be involved in the selection of team members and will assist in the process of creating a team charter (purpose, goals, and guidelines). In some situations, the leader guides the team to its conclusion.

TEAM MEMBERS

A team member, whether part-time or full-time, not only provides specific expertise upon request, but also should be committed to helping the team toward its outcome by observing the norms agreed upon by the group.

---

*See Ideas 4.1–4.6, "Sponsorship Responsibility to Teams."

I D E A

- **Recognize the behavior of HIT members**

WHAT IS A HIGH IMPACT TEAM?

2.5 What Do HIT Members Do?

The research is clear (See Carew,D., Parisi-Carew,E., Blanchard K.; and Katzenback, J.R. and Smith, D.K. as referenced in Idea 19.20). High Impact Team members consistently act differently than members of nonperforming teams:

HIT members view the team's work with excitement and passion; they regard the team's work as important and valuable.

HIT members tend to view the work of the team as a game that must be won in order for the team to succeed.

HIT members view being a member of the team as an honor; they feel they and their colleagues are members of an elite group.

HIT members are initially and ultimately optimistic about the possible outcomes that the team can achieve — even when conditions may not warrant the optimism.

HIT members usually make sacrifices that put work above most of the other aspects of their life for a period of time.

HIT members realize that the solutions for the team's focus cannot be found by one person; team performance will always exceed individual output.

I D E A

WHAT IS A HIGH IMPACT TEAM?

2.6 HIT or Miss?

At this point you may not have a HIT on your hands, but would you know one if you saw one? Consider the following HIT list of team characteristics:

- **Outstanding team performance.** The cumulative effect of individual team member behaviors results in outstanding team performance.
- **Positive morale and esprit de corps.**
- **Processes for tapping into excellence.** HITs have discovered ways of collectively drawing on the skill, knowledge, and effort of individual team members.
- **Technological know-how.** Technological capacity exists in HITs, but also in many mediocre teams. So, technological know-how is a HIT criterion, but it's not necessarily a distinctive one.
- **Work flexibility.** HITs tend to change the way they do their work more frequently than non-HITs.
- **Creative conflict.** HITs view and manage conflict between team members to capitalize on differences.
- **Effective decision making.** HITs use decision-making steps that build on the competence and commitment of *all* team members.
- **Shared leadership.** HITs have shared, flexible leadership responsibilities within the members of the team.
- **Team talk.** HITs usually develop their own language, norms, stories, jokes, and points of view reflecting camaraderie..
- **Outcome oriented.** HITs usually view the outcomes as all-important, which serves as social "grease" to minimize conflicts of ego.
- **Evaluation of results.** HITs continually evaluate their output against their planned outcomes and look for better ways to obtain results.

WORKSHEET

WHAT'S IN IT FOR YOU?

• Learn the work that must be done before creating a HIT

WHAT IS A HIGH IMPACT TEAM?

2.7 Setting the Stage for a HIT

Determine if your team is being set up for success. Check to see if the following preliminary steps have been accomplished:

	Yes	No
1. Someone has effectively created a team charter that states clearly the team's purpose, goals, and guidelines.	❑	❑
2. Someone has chosen team members with diverse, yet complementary technical skills and knowledge.	❑	❑
3. Someone has specified clear mechanisms of team accountability to the organization that spawned the team.	❑	❑
4. Someone has specified a non-team member (for example, a sponsor) not only to deflect the criticism the team may be subjected to, but also to buffer the team from the bureaucratic hassles that arise.	❑	❑
5. Someone has specified an individual who will take the "sting" out of interim failures so that the team is embedded in a culture of learning — not punishment.	❑	❑
6. Someone has selected outcomes that cannot be achieved by one individual or unit. The purpose requires interdependence of team members' efforts.	❑	❑
7. Someone has passionately articulated the meaning of the team's work to the organization's future.	❑	❑
8. Someone has recruited team members based on the criterion that they must be technically competent, but also able to work with others.	❑	❑
9. Someone has recruited individuals based on the criterion that the team member is passionately committed to excellence in the area of the team's focus.	❑	❑

CHAPTER THREE

TYPES OF TEAMS

WHAT'S IN IT FOR YOU?

- **Discover the distinctions between cross-functional teams, work unit teams, management teams, and task force teams**
- **Determine which type of team best suits the overall outcomes you're trying to achieve**
- **Consider if your team should be part-time, full-time, temporary, or long-standing**
- **Understand what functions a self-managed work team is most likely to take on**

The nature of a team is determined by its function and structure. A clear understanding of the type of team you're forming will help you overcome some inevitable pitfalls and lay the groundwork for selecting team members and creating norms, guidelines, and processes. This chapter will help guide you through the determination of the type of team needed to accomplish your tasks and goals.

I D E A

TYPES OF TEAMS

3.1 Four Types of Teams

Teams come in myriad shapes and sizes, but most can be categorized into four types. Which of these types of teams best suits your needs?

CROSS-FUNCTIONAL TEAM

When the purpose and outcomes of the team depend on the insights, expertise, and support of various departments, functions, or organizational interests, a Cross-Functional Team is needed with members representing those various interests. For example:

- A patient-centered hospital team that includes an assigned doctor, nurse, nutritionist, orderly, and accounting rep
- A football team with offensive, defensive, and special team players.

WORK UNIT TEAM

In a Work Unit Team (WUT), members are usually made up of the people who do the work or produce a product within a particular area or department. Examples include:

- Shift of machine operators responsible for producing a unit goal
- A group of workers in finance responsible for reducing the number of days outstanding on customer invoices.

MANAGEMENT TEAM

Management Teams typically consist of leaders of major areas in the organization who have position power and who meet frequently to discuss and solve the organization's problems. Top Management Teams may include both line and staff VPs or directors who have been convened by the CEO, but they rarely include more than two layers of the hierarchy. For example:

- Executive council
- Board of Directors.

TASK FORCE TEAM

A Task Force is usually a large group of people (as many as 20–30) drawn from multiple functions and levels who are temporarily assigned to investigate an issue or problem and make recommendations to top management. What distinguishes a Task Force Team is its temporary nature. Examples include:

- Issue-oriented or problem-solving team
- Group of people assigned to create the organization's vision, mission, and values.

I D E A

- **Build awareness of potential obstacles in Cross-Functional Teams**

TYPES OF TEAMS

3.2 Concerns about Cross-Functional Teams

The very nature of Cross-Functional Teams creates reasons for concern. If you decide to move ahead, keep your eyes open for these possible hazards:

- **Invitation for conflict.** Taking a "cross-slice" of people representing many aspects of the organization may be the very thing necessary to create a new product, develop a process, or achieve an outcome. The different points of view must be present regardless of possible conflict.

- **Not-so-hidden agendas.** The possibility of "silos" of interest can imbue an individual team member with an "agenda" that doesn't serve the team. Individuals from various departments or functions may bring with them their department's interests which they are charged with representing.

- **Territorial behavior.** Individuals in a particular area or department may see the team's goal as their territory and not requiring interdependence among team members.

- **Resource reallocation.** An area or department might be threatened by the team's ability to reallocate resources currently being given to that particular area.

- **Ineffective influence.** An individual team member may only be listening for his or her department or area and not actually have the power to represent it.

- **Power plays.** If different levels of the hierarchy are represented, it could create an uneven power distribution among team members. Typically, in a Cross-Functional Team, all members are of equal value and importance. However, when a vice-president and a line worker are thrown together, the positions may be hard to ignore and could make for an unequal distribution of power — no matter what norms are established by the team.

I D E A

- **Consider steps that can help overcome potential problems of Cross-Functional Teams**
- **Understand the political implications of Cross-Functional Teams**

TYPES OF TEAMS

3.3 Cross-Functional Considerations

An ounce of prethought is worth a ton of afterthought when it comes to a Cross-Functional Team.

Make sure you, as team leader …

- select team members who have credibility and support from members of the organization outside the area they represent
- select team members who are known for their open-mindedness, sense of fair play, and problem-solving ability
- select team members who are passionately interested in the team's project or purpose
- select team members who are indispensable and the most technically competent in their particular area
- are ready to protect the team members from the "political wrath" of their departments by interceding if necessary with their leader
- examine and alleviate possible problems that could be created for an area or department because of the outcomes or goals of the team.

I D E A

• **Understand the limitations of a Work Unit Team**

TYPES OF TEAMS

3.4 Work Unit Team Concerns

The limited nature of a Work Unit Team (WUT) creates built-in liabilities you will need to study and be ready to overcome.

- Membership on a WUT is limited to the people already assigned to the unit and is seldom changed to accommodate the needs of the team. Because the WUT may be less flexible, it may not succeed as a team given the competence, commitment, and composition of the team members.

- Usually a WUT has very little outside perspective. Sometimes the needed expertise to solve a problem is present in the existing membership, and sometimes it's not.

- The scope of WUT projects tends to be limited to narrow work-related problems, but the answer to those problems may be systemic and lie outside the scope or perspective of the team.

- Given the permanence of a WUT, team members may hesitate to deal with the conflict that is a natural by-product of High Impact Teams. The conservative approach would be to keep conflict at a minimum.

- Natural WUTs may, at times, view themselves as the victim of the system or of management. Instead of increasing performance, they may want to band together in an "us against the organization" posture.

- In organizations in which frequent downsizing has occurred, WUT members may see teams as a management ploy to increase output and decrease the labor force.

- In WUTs that have been together for a great length of time, a sense of insularity may have developed that translates into an "if it ain't invented here, it can't be any good" syndrome.

- In many instances, the leadership that sponsors the WUT doesn't want to "trust the institution to the inmates" and fails to empower the WUT to really improve performance.

I D E A

- **Consider ideas for making Work Unit Teams work**

TYPES OF TEAMS

3.5 Eight Considerations for Developing Work Unit Teams

To overcome some of the potential liabilities of a WUT, consider the following ideas:

1. Up front, switch the "in-place" membership by 25% to 50%, insisting upon "cross-integration" of like roles with different people.

2. "Outplace" some team members with other teams for mandatory cross-training.

3. Seed the WUT with outside subject-matter experts (SMEs) who can add new ideas to the team.

4. Provide resources to the team and require members to study how other units solved problems similar to theirs.

5. Empower the WUT to recommend how the system could be changed to improve work unit performance.

6. Don't tolerate an "us" and "them" attitude by overlooking it. Be clear from the beginning that the WUT and the organization are one and the same.

7. Provide team training on what High Impact Teams do and how team members act toward each other.

8. Reward the WUT's efforts and productivity with increased team autonomy by giving members greater budgetary control, and the authority to make selection, hiring, and staffing decisions.

IDEA

WHAT'S IN IT FOR YOU?

• Understand why Management Teams can be difficult

TYPES OF TEAMS

3.6 Management Team Concerns

There are a number of reasons the Management Teams are usually the most difficult to foster and maintain. Here are the difficulties you are most likely to encounter:

- Heavy demands on a top executive's time infringes on consistent attendance and participation.
- Characteristics, such as strong egos and individualism, that have been reinforced in the executive's rise to the top of the organization often run contrary to teamwork.
- Promises made to people they manage may create conflict of interest between loyalty to an individual and the organization.
- The absence of "chemistry" between high-priced would-be CEOs often results in lack of authenticity and true empathy between members.
- The CEO must "give up power" to the team, which is especially hard to do in closely held companies.
- Issues often degenerate into short-term tactical matters rather than focusing on long-term strategic issues that require a comprehensive interdependent outlook from all team members.

I D E A

TYPES OF TEAMS

3.7 Seven Considerations for Management Team Effectiveness

Management Teams can be effective and productive with hard work and focus on process. The process procedures described throughout this book will be critical to observe and follow, but you also need to consider these ideas specific to a Management Team:

1. The CEO does not have to be the permanent team leader. Often leadership can be rotated, or shared, over the life of the team.

2. Outside consultants, process consultants, or internal people can be used to help keep the egos in check and remind the team members of the norms they have agreed upon.

3. Incentives for top executives could be altered to include the outcomes shared by the team. Specific outcomes — besides shareholder value — need to be shared and incentivized at the Management Team level.

4. Although this can bring an additional set of headaches to consider, include people outside the formal top management level who will add a plurality of ideas and balance of perspective.

5. Use subteams within the top management group to get preliminary work accomplished. This strategy will lessen the burden of meeting time for the whole group.

6. Encourage team members to take team responsibilities that require crossing over their formal areas of responsibilities in order to generate a greater understanding and empathy of areas other than their own.

7. Watch your agenda so that most, if not all, items require members to work interdependently rather than being tactically dependent on one particular area.

I D E A

WHAT'S IN IT FOR YOU?

• **Understand when Task Force Teams are most appropriate**

TYPES OF TEAMS

3.8 Situations Requiring Task Forces

A Task Force Team often begets another Task Force Team. Usually, the multiple charges given a task force require a large number of people and force the formulation of smaller teams to actually get the work done. Consider using a Task Force Team in these types of situations:

- Vested interests have not been able to get beyond their secular views in previous attempts.
- The credibility of the findings is important to establish with outside and/or inside stake holders.
- The findings need to be creative, yet free from assumed constraints as much as possible.
- Implementation of recommendations needs to be free from incumbent personnel.

I D E A

WHAT'S IN IT FOR YOU?

• **Understand the true costs of part-time and full-time teams**

TYPES OF TEAMS

3.9 Considerations for Part-Time or Full-Time Teams

A part-time member is someone who does other things besides being on the team and is responsible for output outside the team's output. A full-time team member is paid to do nothing else but the work of the team for a period of time.

Should your team have part-time or full-time team members? The answer depends on money, resources, project goals or purpose, team member skills, importance to the organization, and organizational payoff. It seems, however, that for an important project, full-time teams have the advantage in terms of team member commitment and efficiency.

The table below describes the pros and cons of part-time and full-time teams.

Part-Time Team	Full-Time Team
The combination of team work and other work can lead to burnout.	The opportunity to be mono-focused on one set of outcomes means less likelihood of burnout.
Members could use their "other work" as an excuse for nonproductivity.	There is little or no excuse for team members to be nonproductive because of "other work."
Less expensive to the "lending" department from which the team member comes	More expensive to the "lending" department from which the team member comes
Members have "in and out" behavior from trying to "serve two masters" that could feel like a lack of focus in both settings.	Members have no "in and out" behavior.
Members often do not see the work as a priority for the organization, and the quality of output and timelines may suffer.	Being full-time, members definitely understand that the organization is serious about the team's purpose and outcomes.
Members may not take the time to build the clear purpose, consensus, or trust needed for outstanding productivity.	Members can take the time necessary to build the clear purpose, consensus, or trust needed for outstanding productivity.

I D E A

WHAT'S IN IT FOR YOU?

- **Understand the advantages and disadvantages between a standing, or long-term team, and a temporary team**

TYPES OF TEAMS

3.10 Considerations for Standing Teams vs. Temporary Teams

Do the purpose and outcomes of your team demand a team that will be in place for a long time, or do they require a temporary team that has a foreseeable end?

The function and title of a standing team are usually well known to most company employees — the executive committee, the strategic planning team, or the product development group are common examples. A temporary team is one that will end and has a predetermined scope of work. There are plusses or minuses to be considered for each type of team as indicated below.

A Standing Team...	A Temporary Team...
can follow the status of issues and problems over long periods of time.	can be appointed freely, without being obligated to leaders of departments who may have vested interests.
can grasp the historical factors that influence present-day issues.	can produce work without historical baggage.
can serve as an implementation arm for strategic recommendations.	may not be in operation for the implementation of recommendations, so recommendations could be ignored, never tested, or improved.
can have the time to develop the trust necessary between team members for true collaborative solutions.	may not have or take the time to build the trust necessary for true collaborative solutions.
may have vested interests that are never overcome between members.	can more easily shake up vested interests without worry.
may consist of incumbent members who have little chemistry over time.	may not understand the issues because of no "real" experience living the problems.
could be a bottleneck to creative ideas that are not of particular interest to the team.	can be seen by outside stake holders as impartial.
may be hindered by its past history, resulting in low credibility with factions inside or outside the organization.	doesn't have to live with its recommendation, so the commitment to a "painless" solution could be low.

I D E A

- **Understand why it may be beneficial to have different levels of authority represented on one team**

TYPES OF TEAMS

3.11 Considerations for Multilevel Memberships on Teams

Should your team be staffed with members of unequal levels of authority or position power? Combining vice-presidents and line employees may make for interesting results. The access to different types of information results in different perceptions of a problem, which can help produce a more comprehensive, creative solution.

Consider the following pros and cons of multilevel membership.

Pros of Multilevel Membership	Cons of Multilevel Membership
People from different levels can increase the perspectives on the problem and its solutions.	People with less organizational power may be intimidated by those with more power, at the expense of the project.
Each level becomes educated concerning the problems and perspectives experienced at various other organizational levels.	People with less organizational power may seek to win favor from those with more power, at the expense of the project.
All levels of organizations can work to break down the "we–they" views, which may build up over time.	It takes longer to understand the issues from hierarchical perspectives than it does in homogeneous teams.
Vested interests across departments may be challenged.	Information may leak to different levels of the organization, which may be inappropriate.

I D E A

WHAT'S IN IT FOR YOU?

• **Determine the characteristics of a team through a matrix of choices**

TYPES OF TEAMS

3.12   Team Type Matrix

Full- or part-time? Standing or temporary? Multilevel or homogeneous? To determine each of these choices, you must consider the scope of the team's work and its purpose. The following Team Type Matrix should help in your considerations.

Type of Team	Part- or Full-Time?	Standing or Temporary?	Multilevel or Homogeneous?
Cross-Functional	Part- or Full-Time	Temporary or Standing	Multilevel or Homogeneous
Work Unit	Full-Time	Standing	Homogeneous
Management	Full-Time	Standing	Homogeneous
Task Force	Part- or Full-Time	Temporary	Multilevel

Investigation into organizational teams* indicates 45% of all employees who are members of any team belong to a standing or permanent work team; 30% of those on teams are assigned to temporary project teams; 18% are members of a long-term Cross-Functional Team.

---

*Jack Gordan, "Work Teams: How Far Have They Come?" *Training* (October 1992): 60.

I D E A

• **Learn what functions make a self-managed work team self-managing**

TYPES OF TEAMS

3.13   Self-Managed Work Team

A self-managed work team is a team that does what one person, the manager, traditionally does. It can be cross-functional or "silo-focused" (singularly focused), but it is usually full-time. A self-managed team determines the team's budget, training, hiring, firing, purchasing schedules, performance appraisal, and performance targets. It is the ultimate in employee involvement and motivation.

The most common functions* handled by self-directed work teams are as follows:

1. Work schedules
2. Dealing directly with customers
3. Setting performance targets
4. Training.

The least common functions** are as follows:

1. Firing
2. Hiring
3. Budgeting
4. Performance appraisals.

The biggest mistake organizations make is thinking that self-managed teams are born, not bred. By following the ideas outlined in this book, a team may evolve into self-management. But, it is wise for you to consider the following questions before attempting to create a self-managed HIT:

• How would you know an intact team is ready to handle these functions?
• How do you develop the skills of team members to handle these functions?
• How could you get your managers to help teams manage these functions?
• What would be the reasons not to allow the team to handle these functions?
• What would be the impact of teams never being able to manage any or all of these functions?

---

*Jack Gordan, "Work Teams: How Far Have They Come?" *Training* (October 1992): 63.

**Gordan, ibid., 63.

CHAPTER FOUR

SPONSORSHIP RESPONSIBILITY TO TEAMS

WHAT'S IN IT FOR YOU?

- **Clarify the role and importance of a team sponsor**
- **Learn how sponsorship may be the key to team empowerment**
- **Answer questions that will help you determine a team's boundaries**

As a team leader, you may wonder why there's a need to identify a team sponsor. This chapter attempts to convince you that your team will have a greater sense of its own power and more likelihood of success when it is brokered in the organization by a sponsor. You may actually discover that the team will be better served if you become the sponsor and identify a new team leader.

IDEA

• **Learn what it means to empower a team**

SPONSORSHIP RESPONSIBILITY TO TEAMS

4.1 Sponsorship, the Key to Empowerment?

If an organization holds a team responsible for getting work done, it is also responsible for empowering the team to do the work. *Empowerment* means the sponsor grants or gains for the team both the responsibility and the authority to get work accomplished.

Responsibility means a transfer of obligation to the team to obtain certain outcomes. *Authority* means the capacity to use or spend resources to obtain the desired outcomes. There may be nothing more frustrating than to be granted responsibility without the authority to carry it out. Empowerment creates a "space" for a team to do its work by giving both responsibility and authority.

Sponsors and team leaders need to be clear on the issue of empowerment, and they should be ready to answer questions the team will likely ask:

- What exactly are we responsible for?
- What authority do we have over what we are responsible for?
- What decisions can be made without sponsor approval?
- What resources can be used?
- Why haven't others outside the team been so empowered?
- Will the sponsor override decisions he or she doesn't like or get so involved that the team feels "disempowered" rather than empowered?

I D E A

• **Understand the specific duties of a sponsor**

SPONSORSHIP RESPONSIBILITY TO TEAMS

4.2 The Role of a Sponsor

Being a team sponsor may feel like being a team leader because the sponsor serves the team's outcomes, but the role is very different. As a sponsor, you might be the individual who thought of the team's purpose or the person who authorized the resources. You could be the sponsor of many groups. Specifically, the functions of the sponsor are as follows:

- To clarify the team's purpose to the team
- To help the team understand and comply with its boundaries of authority
- To provide the team with resources needed to obtain the desired results
- To be the team's liaison with the rest of the organization
- To provide information needed by the team
- To represent the team's proposed outcomes to the larger organization
- To aid in the selection of initial team members
- To act as a political advice-giver to the team
- To buffer the team from critics and those who would maintain the status quo
- To reduce the bureaucratic red tape that could prevent the team from implementing truly creative solutions
- To aid the team in obtaining organizational acceptance of the recommendations of the team
- To aid the team in receiving recognition for its efforts.

I D E A

• **Understand how a sponsor sets a team's boundaries**

SPONSORSHIP RESPONSIBILITY TO TEAMS

4.3 A Baker's Dozen: A Boundary-Setting Checklist for Sponsors

A sponsor needs to set a team's boundaries. But how? First, the sponsor must have clarity and understanding about the issue or project the team will be working to solve. The sponsor must weigh business issues against available budget and potential payoff. The boundaries must provide enough latitude for the team to flex its skills and work autonomously at some stage. The team must be given adequate authority to use appropriate resources and make choices that increase its capacity to be effective and implement agreed-upon solutions. After the general boundaries have been established, more detailed boundaries may need to be set.

To determine boundaries, a sponsor needs to answer the following questions:

1. What is the purpose of the team? What are the desired outcomes or deliverables?
2. Are there apparent measures or indicators that define the limits of the team's authority?
3. What cost limits are there?
4. Are there effects that, despite the achievement of desired outcomes, will not be tolerated?
5. Are there organizational values that cannot be violated at any cost or benefit?
6. What timelines for delivery of outcomes cannot be missed?
7. Are there restrictions concerning the utilization of manpower?
8. What sacred cows must be spared?
9. What criteria can the team use to know that it needs to obtain sponsor permission, rather than wait for forgiveness?
10. What business realities should be focused upon, internal and external to the organization, to understand the problem or issue clearly?
11. What are the consequences of nondelivery of outcomes?
12. What incentives are there for the team if outcomes are reached? Exceeded?
13. If the sponsor becomes too involved in the ongoing work of the team, how will the team let the sponsor know?

I D E A

WHAT'S IN IT FOR YOU?

• Become aware of groundwork that a sponsor may need to do before initiating a team or creating a team culture

SPONSORSHIP RESPONSIBILITY TO TEAMS

4.4 Is the Organization Ready for Teams?

If necessary, do you have a plan in mind to introduce the team approach into your organization or unit? As a sponsor, you may have to cultivate the ground before growing your team. You may actually have to prepare the organization to support a team culture. These questions will help you determine how much sowing is needed before reaping the rewards of teams:

- What is the connection between the benefits of teams and the long-range business plans for the organization?
- What changes need to be made in policies, systems, procedures, and structures in order for teams to work in your organization?
- How will you help people in leadership positions react positively to the transference of power required to make High Impact Teams work?
- What training needs to be encouraged in order for the necessary skills to be developed for a team-based culture?
- How will you try to ensure that increased decision-making authority is given to teams as they develop?
- How will you change the incentive system to support a team-based culture?
- Who will decide the composition of the teams you authorize?
- How will you emphasize a performance ethic in a team-based culture?

I D E A

• **Understand the power of a sponsor's vision**

SPONSORSHIP RESPONSIBILITY TO TEAMS

4.5 Vision and Sponsors

How well has the team's purpose and the vision and how it will contribute to the organization been communicated? If the sponsor has not effectively communicated the purpose and vision, it is the team leader's responsibility to make it happen. A team's commitment to its goals is directly connected to how well the sponsor has communicated the common purpose for which the team was created.

Sponsors must believe so passionately in what can be accomplished that they inspire the team to create what is in the sponsor's "mind's eye."

The purpose of the team is the key to the team's energy. It must have meaning that transforms a team member's time from drudgery to desire.

When the composer frees others to make music, the music will always be something that, quite unexpectedly, lifts the composer as well as the players.

Sponsors must let go, to have something come back of its own character and on its own accord.

I D E A

- **Understand the sponsor's considerations in setting up the team**

SPONSORSHIP RESPONSIBILITY TO TEAMS

4.6 Consider the First Five Factors

The sponsor should consider the following five factors of setting up a team, outline broad parameters, and even determine conditions for the outcomes. However, the sponsor must be very careful not to dictate *how* the outcomes can or should be reached. For maximum creativity and commitment from the team, specific solutions should be the sole province of the team and team leader.

INITIAL FACTORS OF SETTING UP A TEAM

- Charter (team purpose, desired outcomes, and operating processes)
- Optimal size of the team
- Selection of team members
- Atmosphere/tone
- Environment/space.

CHAPTER FIVE

INITIATING THE CHARTER

WHAT'S IN IT FOR YOU?

- **Increase your team's chances for long-term success by creating a strong foundation**
- **Learn the six components of a charter**
- **Review a sample charter before initiating your team's**
- **Use worksheets to craft the first two elements of the charter: team purpose and outcomes**

Sometimes you need to slow down to go fast. Taking the time to properly charter your team will help avoid many of the typical pitfalls and obstacles that teams face. In this chapter you will initiate the chartering process by defining the ideals of the team, stating boundaries, establishing key success factors, setting team goals, determining values, and quantifying and qualifying measurements that guide the team's performance. After you have established the foundation, the team itself will complete the chartering process using the guidelines in Chapter 8, Creating the Charter.

I D E A

INITIATING THE CHARTER

5.1 Granting the Team's Right to Do Business

The term *chartering* is borrowed from centuries past, when the king of England would grant land to a deserving individual. When the English came to America, the tradition held fast. The king granted charters over certain lands, empowering individuals with the right to own, farm, and govern the land. In return, the individuals paid the king a percentage of the profits made from the land. In effect, a charter was an agreement granted by the king.

Today, the concept of a king granting favors to others is a bit patronizing, but some of the properties of granting a charter remain helpful in a team culture. While the organization confers certain rights, authority, and resources to the team, the team, in return, is responsible for producing certain results. The process of establishing the relationship of the team to the organization and of the team members to each other is "chartering."

Chartering is absolutely essential for the team's success. It is how the team's scope, goals, norms, and other essential elements for high levels of team performance are defined. Basic questions about purpose, boundaries, goals, responsibilities, operating guidelines, values, rules for interpersonal conduct, and endorsement from the sponsoring organization or unit are defined.

The charter is the blueprint for creating HITs. If your team does not have a charter …

- the team will lack purpose and goal clarity.
- it will increase the likelihood that individual interests will overrule team goals.
- it will increase the possibility of interpersonal conflicts.
- it may result in a lack of team resources.
- it increases the possibilities that the needs of the sponsor will not be met.
- it increases the chances that the sponsor and the team will misuse time, material, and people resources.

I D E A

- **Understand why a formal, written charter is so important**

INITIATING THE CHARTER

5.2 Do You Have a Charter?

Your team may already have the elements of a charter in place. But does your team have a formal, written charter? Like the charter from the king of England, a charter needs to be written down so it can be understood and agreed upon by those it affects. Once the charter is created, team members will continue to refer to it to remind themselves, the organization, and their sponsor of their mutual agreements.

The charter accomplishes the following:

- Establishes guidelines that govern team and individual behavior
- Creates team purpose and goals that are stronger than the interests of individual members
- Gives a baseline against which team outcomes can be measured
- Gives a baseline against which team member behaviors can be assessed
- Provides the team with a self-correction measure
- Results in a document that promotes the aims and principles of a united group
- Defines the boundaries and limitations within which the team must operate.

In essence, the charter sets up the team and sponsor for success, allowing the sponsoring body to empower the team.

I D E A

INITIATING THE CHARTER

5.3 Six Components of a Team Charter

A charter consists of six vital components that should be developed through dialogue among the team sponsor, team leader, and team members.

> 1. Team Purpose
>
> +
>
> 2. Anticipated Team Outcomes
>
> +
>
> 3. Team Responsibilities
>
> +
>
> 4. Team Operating Guidelines
>
> +
>
> 5. Team Norms
>
> +
>
> 6. Charter Endorsement   = Charter

1. **Team Purpose.** The team's purpose is expressed in a purpose statement that answers the questions "Why does a team exist?" and "Why was it formed?" A purpose statement is comprised of an ideal, boundaries, and key success factors.

2. **Anticipated Team Outcomes.** A statement of the team outcomes describes the goals, end results, or deliverables the team is charged with achieving. An outcome statement is comprised of goal, value, and measurement statements.

3. **Team Responsibilities.** The team responsibilities are designated work allocations or defined areas of accountability for which the whole team or individual members are responsible. Responsibility statements can be focused on the whole team, paired individuals, or a single individual.

4. **Team Operating Guidelines.** The operating guidelines are steps or rules that determine how the group does its work. These rules clarify work processes in areas such as meeting structure, problem solving, decision making, and conflict resolution.

5. **Team Norms.** Team norms are guiding principles or rules that govern team members' interpersonal conduct. These rules clarify how people should treat each other.

6. **Charter Endorsement.** Endorsement is the agreement among team members and team sponsor that the charter is appropriate and grants permission for the team to function.

CHARTERING AND COMPULSIVENESS

As you begin the chartering process, do not think that to charter correctly you must do everything described in the sequence outlined. It is preferable that components one and two are initiated prior to convening the team. Components three, four, and five can be accomplished over the first few weeks of the team's existence.

Depending on the type of team and its outcomes, the charter might change somewhat because the group's understanding of the problem increases as the work evolves. Depending on the team, some of the components of the charter will be more relevant than others.

I D E A

• **Determine the best way for you to create the team charter**

INITIATING THE CHARTER

5.4 Recommended and Alternative Ways to Establish the Team Charter

Without a king, there are three ways that a team charter can be established, as described in the chart below.

This book is organized based on alternative 3 — with the sponsor and the team leader initiating the charter and the team members completing it. This recommendation keeps the sponsor separate from the team operations, thus lessening the chances of sponsor domination and increasing team members' commitment to responsibilities, guidelines, and norms. Selecting team members after the purpose and outcomes are formed by the sponsor and team leader allows for more informed recruitment and selection.

Alternative 1	**Alternative 2**	**Alternative 3 (Recommended)**
Sponsor, Team Leader, and Selected Team Members Complete:	Sponsor and Team Leader Complete:	Sponsor and Team Leader Complete:
• Purpose • Outcomes • Responsibilities • Guidelines • Norms • Charter endorsement	• Purpose • Outcomes • Responsibilities • Guidelines • Norms	• Purpose • Outcomes

Alternative 2: **Recruit** | **Select**

• Get team members' endorsement of charter

Alternative 3: **Recruit** | **Select**

Team Leader and Team Members Complete:
• Review of the above
• Responsibilities
• Guidelines
• Norms
• Get charter endorsement from sponsor

Proceed   Proceed   Proceed

IDEA

• **Learn the elements of a purpose statement**

INITIATING THE CHARTER

5.5 The Charter's First Component: The Purpose Statement

The team's purpose statement answers the questions "Why does this team exist?" and "Why was it formed?" The organization or sponsor usually decides the purpose and passes it on to the team leader or team as the team is formed.

There are three elements of a purpose statement:

1. The ideal
2. The boundaries
3. The key success factors

Though short and sweet, the purpose statement is important to frame and specify because …

- it describes the end state for which the team should strive.
- it captures the imagination of team members.
- it appeals to the emotions of team members.
- it serves as a standard by which the team can judge its success.
- it defines the scope of work assigned to the team.
- it defines the team's formal authority and decision-making prerogatives.
- it defines the major things the team must do to avoid no outcomes or poor outcomes.

| **Purpose** | = | Ideal | + | Boundaries | + | Key Success Factors |

I D E A

• **Begin crafting the team's purpose statement by defining the ideal**

INITIATING THE CHARTER

5.6 Defining the Ideal

The first step in drafting a purpose statement is to create the ideal — a clear, concise statement of the end state after it has been reached by the team. The ideal should be expressed in terms of the people or entities that will be affected or served by the team's outcomes or products.

Examples of Statements of the Ideal

- The task force will design and implement a performance review process that the users say is quicker, easier, and more effective than the existing process.
- The team will design a safety system that reduces the total number of fatalities while lowering the cost to the customer.
- The team will merge disparate disciplines into a college program that prepares graduates to exceed employer's expectations in the field of X.
- The team will design and build a prototype X which solves a customer's need to communicate over long distances with another, visually and audibly at lower or present cost to the customer.

Purpose	=	**Ideal**	+	Boundaries	+	Key Success Factors

I D E A

INITIATING THE CHARTER

5.7 Determining Boundaries

Boundary setting, which is done with or by the sponsor, should consist of clear, concise statements concerning policies, procedures, or values that cannot be violated regardless of the outcomes that are produced. Boundaries may take the form of dollar limitations or cost-benefit estimates. Boundaries may also include decision-making guidelines.

Examples of Boundary Statements

- The committee is authorized to spend up to $X$$ to produce the prototype.
- The work unit team may recruit and hire its own personnel with its own budget constraints without prior approval from the sponsor.
- The task force will provide recommendations only after involving those people who will be directly influenced by the recommendation.
- The team must follow organizational policy concerning credit-card use with all travel arrangements.

Purpose	=	Ideal	+	**Boundaries**	+	Key Success Factors

I D E A

- **Complete the purpose statement by establishing the key success factors that can make or break a HIT**

INITIATING THE CHARTER

5.8 Establishing the Key Success Factors

Key success factors are steps, conditions, and givens that must be met or present for the team's work to be considered accomplished or the outcomes obtained.

Sometimes these key success factors are within the team's control; sometimes they are givens that change the team's constraints.

Examples of Key Success Factors

- Supplies for prototype construction must be available by X date or sooner.
- A vendor must be chosen for software programming by mid-June.
- No legislation will be passed governing the distribution of this product for at least five years.
- A project manager must be recruited and hired by 10 June.

| Purpose | = | Ideal | + | Boundaries | + | **Key Success Factors** |

I D E A

WHAT'S IN IT FOR YOU?

- **Learn the elements of team outcomes**

INITIATING THE CHARTER

5.9 The Charter's Second Component: Team Outcomes

The team outcomes should describe the deliverables, end results, or goals the team is charged with achieving. Outcomes should also contain value statements that guide the achievement of the outcomes and the operation of the team. Obviously the goals or results must incorporate key measurements for judging team success.

There are three elements of team outcomes:

1. Goals
2. Value statements
3. Measurements

The team outcomes are important to the team charter because they …

- describe the key deliverables the team is charged with producing.
- describe the values the team will adhere to as it produces its product, outcome, or process.
- describe the tentative measures and standards the team will be striving for to give the team a chance to experience success.
- contain value statements that build team members' emotional commitment to the team's purpose.
- contain measurements against a standard that build a sense of competitiveness.

Outcomes	=	Goals	+	Value Statements	+	Measurements

I D E A

- **Begin crafting team outcomes by setting goals**

INITIATING THE CHARTER

5.10 Setting Team Goals

Goals should be specific, measurable statements of achievable output the team hopes to accomplish. Goals are usually time-bound and can include a list of deliverables.

Examples of Goal Statements

- The task force's work will result in 95% of the company employees evaluated by their manager using the new performance review process by X date.
  — Deliverables
    a. New performance review forms for planning and evaluation of personnel
    b. Training curriculum for two-day workshop to train all personnel on the performance review process
    c. Calendar of events for merging the new performance review process into the budgeting cycle
- The team will demonstrate the new prototype for customer use at 99% reliability and 95% accuracy by X date.
  — Deliverables
    a. 6 prototypes at 3 sites of X, Y, and Z
    b. 6 manuals to aid in future operations
    c. 6 sets of repair kit parts

Outcomes	=	**Goals**	+	Value Statements	+	Measurements

IDEA

WHAT'S IN IT FOR YOU?

• **Decide the value statements that will guide the team outcomes**

INITIATING THE CHARTER

5.11 The Value of Value Statements

A value statement defines the principles that guide how the team goes about achieving its goals. Value statements usually involve conditions of quality, ethics, or human interaction.

Core values set the parameters for the behaviors that are acceptable while the team is busy achieving its outcomes, and they also define the outcomes more fully. For example, the core value "Meeting customer needs while maximizing profits" leads to different decisions and behavior than if the core value were "Exceed customer expectations."

Examples of Value Statements

- The new performance review system will be consistent with the Equal Employment Opportunity guidelines of the U.S. Government and the state of XX.
- The prototype will be safe for customer use and will be produced by an environmentally safe process.
- The project recommendations must involve input from the broadest base of employees to ensure that all points of view are heard.

| Outcomes | = | Goals | + | **Value Statements** | + | Measurements |

I D E A

• **Complete the team outcomes by determining how success will be measured**

INITIATING THE CHARTER

5.12 Measurements of Success

Measurement is the designation of how much and what type of performance the team is trying to produce. Usually measures take the form of quantity (how much/how many), quality (at what level of specification/what level of rejection), timeliness (by when), and cost. The concept of measurement is general at this stage of the chartering process and will get more specific and accurate after the team has had a chance to do its work. The measurements are usually contained in a well-written goal.

If the goal is:

The team will demonstrate the new prototype for customer use at 95% accuracy and 99% reliability by X date at a development cost of no more than $500,000.

The measurements are:

- Quantity = one prototype
- Quality = 95% accuracy and 99% reliability
- Timelines = X date
- Cost = development cost of no more than $500,000

Outcomes	=	Goals	+	Value Statements	+	**Measurements**

I D E A

INITIATING THE CHARTER

5.13 Sample Initial Charter — Purpose and Outcomes

Purpose

Statement of Ideal

- The task force will design, test, and implement a performance review process that the end users say is quicker, easier, and more effective than the existing process.

Statement of Boundaries

- The task force will implement only after involving people who will be directly influenced by the recommendations.
- The performance review process will comply with existing state and federal laws governing the fair treatment of employees.

Key Success Factors

- The task force will implement the review process only after a candidate for Director of Human Resources has been chosen.
- The committee on career development must have its work completed and used by the task force in its preliminary design.

Outcomes

Goals

- The task force implementation will result in 95% of the company employees evaluated by their managers using the new performance review process by X date.
- The task force will deliver new performance review forms, a training curriculum for all personnel on the new review process, and a calendar of events for conversion to the performance review system into the budgeting cycle.

Value Statements

- The new performance review process will be consistent with the company value of showing respect for the individual.
- The new performance review process should hold both the manager and the employee accountable for making the process effective.

Measurements

- Number of employees trained.
- The date by which they are trained.
- An employee satisfaction survey normally done by the company every three years.

W O R K S H E E T

WHAT'S IN IT FOR YOU?

- Craft the initial charter's purpose statements by using the forms and guidance given to record preliminary thoughts. These thoughts will be used by the selected team members when creating the full charter.

INITIATING THE CHARTER

5.14 Initial Purpose Statement

Team: _____

Sponsor: _____

Team Leader: _____

Purpose

Statement of Ideal

(What does it look like if the end state is reached from the point of view of those the team is serving or affecting?) _____

_____

_____

_____

Boundary Statements

(What policies, procedures, or values cannot be violated no matter what outcomes are produced?) _____

_____

_____

_____

Key Success Factors

(What are the steps, conditions, or givens that must be present for the team's work to be considered accomplished or the outcomes achieved?) _____

_____

_____

_____

W O R K S H E E T

WHAT'S IN IT FOR YOU?

• Craft the initial charter's statement of outcome by using the forms and guidance given to record preliminary thoughts. These thoughts will be used by the selected team members when creating the full charter.

INITIATING THE CHARTER

5.15 Initial Statement of Outcomes

Team: _____

Sponsor:_____

Team Leader: _____

Outcomes
Goals
(What specific and measurable output does the team hope to accomplish?)

_____

_____

_____

_____

Value Statements
(What does acceptable behavior look like as the team does its work?)

_____

_____

_____

_____

Measurements
(How would you quantify and qualify the team's output so you can tell if it has accomplished what it set out to accomplish?) _____

_____

_____

_____

_____

CHAPTER SIX

OPTIMAL TEAM SIZE AND SELECTION OF TEAM MEMBERS

WHAT'S IN IT FOR YOU?

- Learn how many people are needed for maximum team performance
- Recruit team members with the characteristics that help ensure HITs
- Interview candidates with questions designed to reveal competence and commitment to team membership
- "Sell" potential members by projecting team benefits in a way that appeals to their values

Once the team purpose and outcomes are determined, the next important step in creating a HIT is the selection of team members. Often this is done by selecting obvious choices, or throwing everyone together and hoping for the best. This chapter will help you determine who and what you need represented on your team, and then how to go about attracting them.

IDEA

• **Learn how many, or how few, people it takes to create a HIT**

OPTIMAL TEAM SIZE AND SELECTION OF TEAM MEMBERS

6.1 Optimal Size of Teams

Once you have initiated the charter, the next step is to recruit and select your team members. But, how many? Too many people on a team is unproductive. Not enough people on a team is also unproductive. The specific number of people you choose for a team depends, of course, on the type of team and the scope and complexity of the project. However, for reasonable productivity, the minimum size for a team is four people; the maximum is 12.* The optimal size of a HIT for the best output is eight to nine people.

The size of a team is important for the following reasons:

- Recent research shows significant drops in output and quality of team interactions when there are more than 12 members on a team.*

- The beauty of teams lies in the diversity of viewpoints. Diversity is best served by more than three people.

- A group of people can bring more to problem solving than an individual typically does.

- Teams composed with task interdependence in mind will seldom exceed 12 people.

- Teams comprised of more than 12 people often result in duplication of expertise and resources.

---

*Jon R. Katzenback and Douglas K. Smith, *The Wisdom of Teams: Creating the High-Performance Organization* (New York: Harper Business, 1993), p. 275.

I D E A

• **Learn why teams larger than 12 to 13 people are not optimal**

OPTIMAL TEAM SIZE AND SELECTION OF TEAM MEMBERS

6.2 Six Reasons Why Big* Isn't Always Better

While it may seem "the more, the merrier," that is definitely not the case in a team setting.

1. Achieving a common understanding and consensus of purpose, values, and work procedures becomes problematic in a large group.

2. It is difficult for team members to be heard or have the necessary "air time" to advocate or explore their issues in a large group.

3. Often, subgroups or interest blocs form because the group is too large for issues to be fully developed or explored.

4. Because of lack of time, large groups seldom develop the interpersonal closeness that is characteristic of HITs.

5. Large groups tend to revert back to a traditional way of working that responds to a hierarchical manager who makes decisions.

6. Team members who have a strong need to perform tend to approach teaming by forming subteams to meet performance requirements.

---

*Big = more than 12 or 13 people.

I D E A

• **Learn why three or fewer people on a team is not optimal**

OPTIMAL TEAM SIZE AND SELECTION OF TEAM MEMBERS

6.3 Six Reasons Why Good Things Don't Always Come from Small* Teams

Depending on the charge of the team, too few people can be a distinct liability to a team's efforts.

1. There may not be enough members to do the work or accomplish the team outcomes.
2. There may not be enough technical expertise to accomplish the team outcomes.
3. There may not be enough diversity of ideas, experience, or viewpoints to reach truly creative solutions.
4. Small teams may not have enough members to "sell" the team's outcomes to the rest of the organization.
5. Personalities of individual members play a bigger and disproportionate role in the team's performance.
6. The number and quality of individual learning possibilities are greatly reduced.

*Small = Three or fewer people.

I D E A

• **Understand the importance of recruitment and selection**

OPTIMAL TEAM SIZE AND SELECTION OF TEAM MEMBERS

6.4 Recruitment and Selection

Whether you have a wide range or limited number of choices from which to recruit your team members, it is important to understand that "to build a strong house you must lay a strong foundation."

Recruitment and selection must be thoughtfully done for the following reasons:

- The right mix of technical talent must be present in order for work to be accomplished.
- Technical expertise is no substitute for the interpersonal skills necessary to bring out the motivation and excitement in others. In fact, technical expertise and human understanding might be inversely correlated in some people.
- Plurality of ideas and diversity in thinking is more important in groundbreaking groups, research and development groups, multinational groups, and cross-functional teams. But without some diversity, all groups may suffer from the inability to respond creatively to the purpose of the team.
- There seems to be a correlation between higher output (one-third more) in organizations that have optimistic workers than in those with nonoptimistic workers. You want team members who can think they will create something helpful or innovative. Pessimistic people don't tend to have those dreams.
- Prospective team members must have a passion for the outcomes the team is charged with producing. The quality of work produced by a team is directly connected to the amount of "fire in the bellies" of the team members asked to produce that work.

WORKSHEET

WHAT'S IN IT FOR YOU?

• **Recruit team members who have the potential for creating a HIT**

OPTIMAL TEAM SIZE AND SELECTION OF TEAM MEMBERS

6.5 Ten Qualities of Prospective Recruits

Compare each recruit to the characteristics listed below. The higher the potential team member's score, the greater the chance that recruitment will be successful. These considerations may be contingent upon the type, size, and expectations for the team.

No = 1   **Yes** = 2

_____ 1. Does the person complement or better me in intelligence, expertise, interpersonal skills, or desire?

_____ 2. Has the person demonstrated a passion for excellence (in the area of the team's outcomes)?

_____ 3. Has the person demonstrated an ability to work with others?

_____ 4. Does the person have an incredibly strong appetite for new ideas? Does the person have a hungry mind?

_____ 5. Does the person show an optimistic attitude toward what he or she can accomplish?

_____ 6. Does the person question the givens to find limit-breaking solutions?

_____ 7. Is the person willing to make a sacrifice of a "normal" life because of the passion he or she has for the challenge of the group?

_____ 8. Does the person feel the process of discovery is its own reward?

_____ 9. Is the person interested in being a team member because of a love for the work or the project?

Rule Busters = 1   **Insiders** = 2

_____ 10. Are the people I've chosen "insiders," motivated to succeed within the system, or are they "rule busters" who march to their own drummer?

WORKSHEET

- Discover a series of interview questions that will help you tap a recruit's potential to be a team member

OPTIMAL TEAM SIZE AND SELECTION OF TEAM MEMBERS

6.6 Questions to the Candidate: Setting the Context in Selection

Your options may not always be flexible, but there seem to be clear, proven ideas that lead to effective team member selection. Consider asking each of your potential team members the following questions:

1. What work (other) involvement would you be willing to renounce or delegate if you were to become a team member?

2. How did you hear of the opportunity to be a team member? (This question can demonstrate that the recruit knows where to find the cutting-edge information.)

3. Describe an instance in which you made a creative connection with seemingly unrelated ideas. (You may need to provide your own example to stimulate the candidate's own recollection.)

4. Describe a broad set of interests you have. (You are looking for people who not only are talented and intelligent, but also have multiple frames of reference.)

5. Describe a circumstance in which you had to work with someone you didn't like or with whom you didn't get along. What did you do to resolve it?

6. Describe how being a part of this team relates to your personal goals.

7. Describe a time when you experienced being part of a team or group that did truly innovative work.

I D E A

WHAT'S IN IT FOR YOU?

• Learn what you need to project about the team in order to attract the best team members

OPTIMAL TEAM SIZE AND SELECTION OF TEAM MEMBERS

6.7 Ten Tips for Recruiting for Teams

More often than not, the talented workers of today will opt for autonomy rather than working in a team. The way to "sell" reticent potential team members is to make sure of the following:

1. They perceive the work as irresistibly innovative and cutting edge.
2. They see those on the team as the best, the elite.
3. They can be seen as one of the best and the brightest.
4. They can access leading-edge technology, processes, or ideas.
5. They can clearly see how the work will benefit the organization.
6. They can clearly see how they can use their gifts.
7. They can clearly understand how the team's work is free from bureaucratic hassle and red tape.
8. They can see that the organization has thoughtfully provided the necessary resources.
9. Their spirit of discovery can be stimulated in a group context.
10. They are led, not managed. (In other words, they are not told what to do or micromanaged, but they see leadership as fluid, evolving, and dependent entirely on competency, project knowledge, and interpersonal skills.)

IDEA

OPTIMAL TEAM SIZE AND SELECTION OF TEAM MEMBERS

6.8 Ten Things That Drive People Crazy on Teams

1. **Poor leadership.** The team leader fails to monitor and keep things moving in the appropriate direction.

2. **Goals are unclear.** Members are not really sure what they are trying to accomplish.

3. **Assignments are not taken seriously by team members.** There seems to be no preparation for or by team members.

4. **Lack of action plans.** The team's meetings are not focused; discussions stray from the subject. "What are we supposed to be doing today?"

5. **Wasteful meetings.** Meetings are a waste of time, with unproductive resolution of issues and no conclusions or decisions made.

6. **Irresponsible participants.** Team members do not follow through or keep their promises (with work to be done).

7. **One person or clique dominates.** Some members talk and push for their positions while others wonder why they are there.

8. **No preparation.** There is a lack of meeting structure, no agenda, and the materials and things that really need to be at the meeting somehow are not there. Someone has not done his or her homework.

9. **Hidden agendas or personal axes to grind.** Some team members are closed to other points of view.

10. **Lack of regard by management.** Recommendations of the team are often ignored by the management that appointed the team in the first place.

I D E A

OPTIMAL TEAM SIZE AND SELECTION OF TEAM MEMBERS

6.9 A Dozen Things People Like About Teams That Function Well

1. The team knows what it is supposed to do and what its goals are.
2. Meeting time is carefully controlled. The meeting starts on time and ends on time. Enough time is allowed to get the work done.
3. People are sensitive to each other's needs and feelings.
4. People listen to and respect the opinions of others.
5. Meetings are characterized by an informal, relaxed atmosphere rather than a formal exchange.
6. There is good preparation on the part of the leader and members.
7. Team members are seen as skillful and passionate about the problem or issue the group is working on.
8. Interruptions are avoided or kept to a minimum.
9. Minutes or records are kept, so ground is not covered again and again.
10. Periodically the team stops to appraise its own process. Needed adjustments are made.
11. Team members feel recognized and appreciated for their contributions.
12. The work of the team is accepted and used and seems to make a significant contribution to the organization.

I D E A

WHAT'S IN IT FOR YOU?

- **Identify who should be making the decisions about team member selection**

OPTIMAL TEAM SIZE AND SELECTION OF TEAM MEMBERS

6.10 Who Selects Team Members?

There are three basic ways team members are chosen:

1. The sponsor decides.
2. The team leader decides.
3. The sponsor and team leader decide.

Consider the pros and cons of each alternative, given your team's particular situation, then decide who chooses your team members.

Sponsor Chooses

Pros
- A team is chosen in keeping with sponsor vision
- Friends or supporters of the team leader may not be chosen
- Sponsor support may be more forthcoming when the sponsor chooses

Cons
- One person choosing may lead to ineffective or inappropriate choices
- Friends or supporters of the sponsor could be chosen
- May be seen by outside stake holders as not credible
- May not have the expertise to know which skills are needed to work best on a problem

Leader Chooses

Pros
- The team leader knows whom he/she can work with best
- The leader may feel more responsibility and commitment for the team's outcomes

Cons
- One person choosing may lead to ineffective or inappropriate choices
- Friends or supporters of the team leader could be chosen
- May not know enough about the project vision to choose wisely

Both Leader and Sponsor Choose

Pros
- Both people's strengths and skills are used to make the choices
- Both become committed to the team and its members
- Each could keep the other "honest" regarding why an individual was chosen

Cons
- May lead to conflicts that start the project off on the wrong foot

I D E A

• **Determine who should select new or replacement team members**

OPTIMAL TEAM SIZE AND SELECTION OF TEAM MEMBERS

6.11 Team Members as Recruiters or Selectors

If your team is already in place and the membership must be increased or members replaced, it may be appropriate to let the team choose its new members.
As always, you must consider the "pros and cons" of the approach.

Pros	Cons
The team is the best judge of *what* skills are needed	The team may recruit someone of a like "mind-set" without regard for diversity
The team may be the best judge of *who* has the skills needed	The team will see itself as too autonomous and free of the necessary constraints
The team can be the best ambassador for the team's purpose, outcomes, guidelines, and norms	The team may have no sense of the vision or purpose and will consequently choose someone who will be inappropriate or unacceptable to the sponsor
The team will have a stake in the new team member's success	
It will enhance the team's sense of self-determination	

CHAPTER SEVEN

ENVIRONMENT AND ATMOSPHERE

WHAT'S IN IT FOR YOU?

- **Consider how physical surroundings impact a team's work effectiveness**
- **Realize the importance of "extras" that pay off in productivity and loyalty**
- **Evaluate the emotional tone and "health" of the team**

Because groups of people meeting together gets expensive, the approach is often to cut back on amenities. This may be penny-wise, pound foolish. This chapter builds a case for selecting meeting places free of distractions that discourage productivity, allocating resources appropriately and providing food and drink that feed the brain, not just the stomach. You will also complete two checklists to help you determine the emotional health of your team — an essential to creating an atmosphere for great work.

IDEA

- **Understand the importance of *where* your team meets**

ENVIRONMENT AND ATMOSPHERE

7.1 Why Teams Need a Special Environment

A team's workspace is of prime importance. Why?

- Teams need to be free from distractions.
- A transient space used by others can cause loss of continuity because team materials are disturbed and must be repeatedly reestablished.
- The space a team uses conveys a sense of organizational worth to the team members.
- Having a designated space legitimizes the full concentration of all team members.
- A designated space allows for 24-hour use and access without work-flow interruption.
- With its own space, a team can promote its own separate culture in which great things can happen.
- A separate space keeps organizational interference at a distance.
- A special space will promote single-minded focus on the team purpose and outcomes.

A team's workspace can be ineffective for a variety of reasons:

- The space chosen is too remote to tap organizational resources.
- The space is so visible that outside organizational members become alarmed or concerned with the team's different work habits.
- The space is actually too esthetically stimulating to the extent that it becomes a distraction to team members.
- The space chosen does not contain the cutting-edge technology necessary to communicate or create the team's product or outcome.
- The space is inadequate. For example, the teams that produce actual working prototype products may not have the space to meet the demands of the prototype.

I D E A

WHAT'S IN IT FOR YOU?

- **Create a stimulating working environment**

ENVIRONMENT AND ATMOSPHERE

7.2 How to Create a Team Environment That Works

1. Create surroundings that are esthetically pleasing, but more bland (not bleak) than grand because team members shouldn't be spending time thinking about their surroundings.
2. Select a space that is somewhat isolated, "off the beaten track," but accessible.
3. Have all the tools necessary for the group to do its work.
4. Have access to cutting-edge technology.
5. Allow for different dress codes, hours, and freedom from arbitrary regulations that prevent total team member focus.
6. Create a space that can be modified to suit team outcomes and phases of work.
7. Designate a space that allows the team privacy to ebb and flow, to build creative tension, and to create its own world, with its own language, history, customs, jokes, rituals, and secrets.
8. Select a space that allows freedom from trivial duties, obligations, and workplace nonessentials.
9. Provide enhancements to productivity such as a CD player for background music (Mozart makes you smarter), room for stretching, and places to get outside. Consider an aromatherapy diffuser or some way to freshen the air. Studies indicate 20% and higher levels of productivity when essences fill the air, especially peppermint.*

*Journal of Applied Social Psychology 24: 1179–1203.

IDEA

• **Be prepared to provide your team with the resources it needs**

ENVIRONMENT AND ATMOSPHERE

7.3 Seven Team Resource Considerations

Creating an optimal environment also means providing adequate resources. Resources may include any or all of the following:

1. Make available the services of appropriate outside experts who can be periodically used by the team.

2. Depending upon need, anticipate the use of computers, fax machines, typing services, or phones.

3. Depending upon the team outcomes, anticipate possible travel costs.

4. Depending upon the team outcomes, anticipate the use of temporary help.

5. Depending upon the type and purpose of the team, it may be necessary for team members to modify the obligations they have to their regular organizational jobs, and for the team leader to broker those modified obligations with those to whom they report.

6. When appropriate, give an estimate of how long the team members and those to whom they report can expect the modified arrangement to last.

7. Plan for costs and duration to be 25% higher than anticipated because research studies on teams show they can be expensive.

I D E A

WHAT'S IN IT FOR YOU?

- Consider the "little extras" that can make a huge difference in productivity and morale

ENVIRONMENT AND ATMOSPHERE

7.4 Eat, Drink, and Get to Work

A major fallacy in the workplace today is that if people work longer hours they produce more. Not only does the law of diminishing returns negate that theory, but also our tendency to work long hours without refreshment or attention to our physical needs contributes to our lowered productivity. Value for money, a bagel and cream cheese is a wise investment. The cost of food and drink may be worth it to send a message to team members that says the organization wants to provide a nurturing environment.

- Provide tea, coffee, juices, or bottled water for meetings scheduled to last longer than two hours. Optimal learning studies show significant increases in attention and retention levels when water is sipped during sessions.

- With early morning team meetings at which the team members start their day, when the meeting is scheduled to last longer than two hours, consider providing some form of snack or food — that isn't doughnuts.

- When food is served, the most nutritious foods are fresh fruits, nuts, yogurt, low-fat cottage cheese, bagels, and graham crackers. Avoid high sugar or fat content that creates unstable energy and interferes with people's thought processes.

I D E A

- **Increase awareness of signals that reflect where your team members are emotionally**

ENVIRONMENT AND ATMOSPHERE

7.5 Emotional Tone in Teams

Atmosphere is the emotional tone or ambiance that pervades the team meetings. It is reflected in people's attitudes, posture, facial expressions, and dress. It is crucial for team leaders to monitor the team atmosphere.

- Atmosphere is an indicator of the team members' affect — or their emotional tone. Emotion is a barometer of long-term commitment. While many people can perform even though their heart is not in the task, they rarely do so at peak levels for long periods of time.
- A negative atmosphere is often a precursor of interpersonal problems among team members.
- Atmosphere is often a test of the team's resilience — to see the issue clearly, yet stay optimistic.
- Atmosphere can often show what politically correct behaviors won't.

Ask yourself these questions as you study the atmosphere surrounding your team:

- What signs are there that people are productive?
- What signs are there that people are happy, involved, or participating?
- What sense is there that team members are passionately, yet playfully, motivated to accomplish the team's outcomes?

W O R K S H E E T

WHAT'S IN IT FOR YOU?

• Take the opportunity to diagnose the atmosphere of your team

ENVIRONMENT AND ATMOSPHERE

7.6 The Healthy Atmosphere Checklist

Check Yes or No to the following questions based upon your perceptions of your team meetings.

	Yes	No
• Is there some evidence of playfulness among team members?	❑	❑
• Is there a use of a team language?	❑	❑
• Is there open, honest, respectful dissent among team members?	❑	❑
• Do people smile more than they frown during team meetings?	❑	❑
• Is there a sense that the team can produce something great?	❑	❑
• Is there open affection appropriately shown to team members?	❑	❑
• Is there evidence of past or future productivity from group efforts?	❑	❑
• Is there evidence of "out of the box" thinking?	❑	❑
• Do team members "question the givens" by asking "Why?"	❑	❑
• Is it OK for team members to "break set" and take mini-breaks during work sessions?	❑	❑

If you checked six or more answers in the Yes column, your team has a healthy atmosphere. If you had fewer than six in the Yes column, perhaps you should rate your team on the next checklist — The Unhealthy Atmosphere Checklist.

W O R K S H E E T

WHAT'S IN IT FOR YOU?

- **Discover if your team has an unhealthy atmosphere**

ENVIRONMENT AND ATMOSPHERE

7.7 The Unhealthy Atmosphere Checklist

Check Yes or No to the following questions based upon your perceptions of your team meetings.

	Yes	No
• Do people frequently cry during meetings?	❏	❏
• Do people call other team members after the meetings to discuss what happened at the team meetings?	❏	❏
• Do people defer to the formal leader?	❏	❏
• Do people often not believe their formal leader?	❏	❏
• Are team members just going through the "motions" and really don't believe change is possible?	❏	❏
• Are team members asking to step off the team?	❏	❏
• Are people saying they don't have the time to get the work done?	❏	❏
• Are people "subgrouping" and banding together in team meetings?	❏	❏
• Are people whispering in the "corners of the organization" what can't be said in team meetings?	❏	❏
• Is there an unstated agreement that factions within the team are "really" making the decisions?	❏	❏

If you have five or more checks in the Yes column, you probably don't have a healthy team atmosphere. It would be prudent to create team operating guidelines and norms (Ideas 8.6–8.14) or revisit existing guidelines and norms. You should also find the Ideas, Worksheets, and Assessments in Section 2 helpful.

CHAPTER EIGHT

CREATING THE CHARTER

WHAT'S IN IT FOR YOU?

- Involve team members in the completion of the team charter
- Focus the team on creating guidelines and norms from a process perspective
- Generate ideas for team operating guidelines and norms
- Clarify collective, paired, and individual responsibilities
- Appoint individual responsibilities including meeting leader, process observer, and scribe
- Complete the charter through team and sponsor endorsements
- Communicate the charter to the organization

Completing the team charter may take days as opposed to weeks, but consider it an investment of your team's time. This chapter provides the definitions, examples, and worksheets to guide your team through the nine steps of creating the charter that you and/or the team sponsor initiated.

IDEA

• **Take beginning steps with team members to create the charter**

CREATING THE CHARTER

8.1 Nine Steps for Creating a Team Charter

You will need to lead the team through the subsequent steps of creating a charter as described below.

1. Outline and define the components of a team charter, referring back to Ideas 5.1–5.15, "Initiating the Charter," if necessary:
   • Team purpose; team outcomes; team operating guidelines; team norms; team responsibilities; charter endorsement

2. Review the initial charter's purpose statement (ideal, boundaries, key success factors) and outcome statement (goals, value statements, and measurements) that were written by the sponsor and team leader.

3. Tell the team that the initial purpose and outcome statements are subject to negotiation with the sponsor.

4. Ask the team to draft or redraft the purpose statements and outcome statements that will be discussed during the charter endorsement. (See Worksheets 8.2 and 8.3.)

5. After the purpose and outcome statements are completed, ask them to determine team responsibilities using Ideas 8.15–8.23 and Worksheet 8.24.

6. Next, ask the team to determine team operating guidelines using Ideas 8.6–8.8 and Worksheet 8.9.

7. Then, ask them to determine team norms using Ideas 8.10–8.13 and Worksheet 8.14.

8. Finally, have the team endorse the charter using Idea 8.25 and Worksheet 8.26, before presenting it to the sponsor for endorsement.

9. To bring closure to the charter process, communicate the charter to the organization using Idea 8.28.

WORKSHEET

WHAT'S IN IT FOR YOU?

• **Help team members create a purpose statement**

CREATING THE CHARTER

8.2 The Purpose Statement

Ask team members to consider the initial purpose statement drafted by the sponsor and team leader. Using this worksheet, have them question, clarify, and redraft the statement if necessary.

Initial **Statement of Ideal:**

(Transfer from "Initiating the Charter," Worksheet 5.14.)
(A clear statement of what it looks like if idea is reached) _____

_____

_____

• Points of concern _____

_____

• Questions for clarification _____

_____

• Additional points to be included _____

_____

Recommended Statement of Ideal: _____

_____

_____

Initial **Boundary Statements:**

(Transfer from "Initiating the Charter," Worksheet 5.14.)
(Clear statements concerning policies, procedures, or values that cannot be violated no matter what outcomes are reached) _____

_____

_____

- Points of concern _____
  _____

- Questions for clarification _____
  _____

- Additional points to be included _____
  _____

Recommended Boundaries: _____
_____
_____

Initial Key Success Factors

(Transfer from "Initiating the Charter," Worksheet 5.14.)
(Clear statements of conditions which must be present for the outcome to be met)

_____
_____
_____

- Points of concern _____
  _____

- Questions for clarification _____
  _____

- Additional points to be included _____
  _____

Recommended Key Success Factors: _____
_____
_____

W O R K S H E E T

WHAT'S IN IT FOR YOU?

• **Help team members create a statement of outcomes**

CREATING THE CHARTER

8.3 The Statement of Outcomes

Ask team members to consider the initial statement of outcomes drafted by the sponsor and team leader. Using this worksheet, have them question, clarify, and redraft the statement if necessary.

Initial Goals:

(Transfer from "Initiating the Charter," Worksheet 5.15.)
(Clear statement of achievable output or deliverables for which the team will be held accountable) _____

_____

_____

• Points of concern _____

_____

• Questions for clarification _____

_____

• Additional points to be included _____

_____

Recommended Goals: _____

_____

_____

Initial Value Statements:

(Transfer from "Initiating the Charter," Worksheet 5.15.)
(A definition of specific principles intended to guide how the goal should be reached)

_____

_____

_____

- Points of concern _____
_____

- Questions for clarification _____
_____

- Additional points to be included _____
_____

Recommended Value Statements: _____
_____
_____

Initial Measurements:

(Transfer from "Initiating the Charter," Worksheet 5.15.)
(Statements of how much, how many, what quality, and by what time the goal is to
be reached)_____
_____
_____

- Points of concern _____
_____

- Questions for clarification _____
_____

- Additional points to be included _____
_____

Recommended Measurements: _____
_____
_____

IDEA

WHAT'S IN IT FOR YOU?

- **Discover two perspectives a team leader must have**
- **Understand why the process perspective is so crucial to HITs**
- **Learn the two types of process perspectives and their differences**

CREATING THE CHARTER

8.4 Product and Process Perspectives

Every team needs rules that define and govern how the group will go about doing its work. These are different from the outcomes or ends of the team; they are the means by which those ends are achieved.

HITs separate, but find balance between the two perspectives: product perspective and process perspective.

The **product perspective** is the "What" of the interaction.

- What is the topic?
- What is being done?
- What actions will or could be taken?
- Refer to the purpose and outcomes as stated in the charter (Worksheets 8.2 and 8.3).

The **process perspective** is the "How" of the interaction.

- How are conflicts resolved, problems solved, or decisions made?
- How are the team members relating to each other as they do the work?

In a team situation, both elements are important:

- To focus solely on product perspective may ignore the feelings of anger, fear, isolation, or dissatisfaction that may be generated in team members.
- Attention to the process perspective alone may result in "good feelings," but it also may result in inadequate emphasis on the outcomes that must be achieved.
- Without the product perspective, a lack of team outcomes may result in an organization with a weakened capacity to survive in the marketplace.
- Process issues are the biggest cause of team failure.

I D E A

• **Increase your understanding of product and process perspectives**

CREATING THE CHARTER

8.5 Examples of Product and Process Perspectives

A football team will have a product perspective that might be to have a winning season, operate within a specified budget, generate a certain attendance at home games, etc. These interactions receive much attention from the owner, managers, and coaches.

What might not get as much attention is the team's process perspectives, which are actually independent of the work the team is doing yet vital to it — for example, their relationships to each other or the press. The process perspective includes operating guidelines and team norms that govern the interactions of the team members and will ultimately help the team function as a well-oiled machine.

Even though both operating guidelines and team norms help the team get its work done in a more effective and satisfying manner, there are differences between them. An **operating guideline** is a formal set of procedures to facilitate the work the team is doing. For example, a system or strategy for solving problems is an operating guideline.

Operating guidelines for a football team might include the following:
- At team meetings, final decisions about blocking assignments will be made by the offensive line coach.
- All plays will be called by the offensive coordinator and sent in to the quarterback.
- Game films will be reviewed every Monday.
- If your playbook is lost or misplaced, you are to notify the head coach immediately and make every effort to retrieve it!

A **team norm** describes the way team members will treat each other interpersonally. Team norms for a football team might be as follows:
- Do not avoid conflict, but learn from it.
- Don't talk about another team member behind his back.
- Don't talk to the press negatively about another team member.
- We will openly discuss and solve problems before moving on to another topic.

I D E A

• **Understand why operating guidelines are an important part of the charter**

CREATING THE CHARTER

8.6 Team Operating Guidelines

The primary areas for which guidelines should be developed are meeting structure, problem solving, decision making, and conflict resolution.

Operating Guidelines are critical for the team to create because:

- Without the structure of these procedures, team members may not get the work done.
- The absence of clear guidelines creates conflict among team members.
- The way decisions are made — for example, decision making by consensus — is crucial to continued team member commitment.
- Operating guidelines increase team member satisfaction by reducing ambiguity.
- When guidelines are in place and agreed upon, they save the team time.

Operating guidelines may be ineffective in the following situations:

- The team leader is dominating.
- There is no commitment to be a team.

Use Ideas 8.6 to 8.8 to help determine your team's agreed-upon and formalized operating guidelines. For more detailed information, see the Ideas in Section 2 listed below:

1. How will the team conduct its meetings? (Ideas 9.1–9.16, "Meeting Structure")
2. How will the group solve the problems it encounters? (Ideas 10.1–10.17, "Problem Solving")
3. How will the team make decisions? (Ideas 11.1–11.7, "Decision Making Strategies")
4. How will the team address and resolve conflict? (Ideas 12.1–12.14, "Conflict Resolution Strategies")

Operating Guidelines

I D E A

• **Question the existence and effectiveness of your team's operating guidelines**

CREATING THE CHARTER

8.7 Seven Questions About Your Team's Operating Guidelines

As team leader, you need to know the answers to the following questions. If you don't, or if the answers are vague, work with your team members to better define the operating guidelines. (See Worksheet 8.9, "Establishment of Team Operating Guidelines.")

1. What are the team's meeting guidelines? How shall the meetings be run?
2. What are team members' roles and responsibilities during meetings? Who will lead, facilitate, observe process, record, and keep time?
3. If outcomes or goals have changed or shifted as the team got into action, have they been clearly rewritten?
4. Has the team chosen a problem-solving method and decision-making process? How will problems be solved? How will decisions be made?
5. Has the team designated project work roles and responsibilities? Who will accomplish what, when, and how?
6. Has the team defined project improvement strategies? How will the team change things that are not getting results? How will the team handle changes within/outside the team?
7. Have evaluation strategies been defined? How will project effectiveness be judged?

Operating Guidelines

I D E A

• **Examine examples of operating guidelines to help in establishing your own**

CREATING THE CHARTER

8.8 Examples of a HIT's Operating Guidelines

1. **Involvement.** There will be constant dialogue and discussion by all team members concerning the task, outcomes, activities, and process. All team members will participate and are outcome oriented.

2. **Clear outcomes.** The outcomes of the team will be well understood by all team members. All team members not only understand the outcomes, but also should be passionately committed to them.

3. **Resolve conflict.** Team members will be comfortable with disagreement and understand that conflict is a natural by-product of creativity and passion. Team members don't avoid conflict or try to dominate the discussion. If conflict cannot be resolved, they do not allow it to block group efforts.

4. **Consensus decisions.** Most of the team's decisions are reached by consensus. Team members make their opposition public, instead of hiding it and sabotaging the consensus.

5. **Examine process.** Most of the team members are aware of the team's process. When the team or various team members violate the agreed-upon process norms, attention will be focused on how that violation interferes with team outcomes.

6. **Solve problems.** The team will use a five-step process of problem solving.*

7. **Consensus alternative.** The team will make most of its decisions by consensus. In the event that is not possible, a vote will be taken, and the majority will rule.

Operating Guidelines

*See Ideas 10.1–10.19, "Problem Solving."

W O R K S H E E T

WHAT'S IN IT FOR YOU?

• **Generate ideas from team members for the operating guidelines**

CREATING THE CHARTER

8.9 Establishment of Team Operating Guidelines

Ask each team member to respond to the questions below. Use the worksheets as a reference when the whole team discusses and reaches decisions on operating guidelines.

1. Have program outcomes and milestones changed since the sponsor and team leader statements in the initial charter?

   _____

2. How should team meetings be run? Should agendas and minutes be used? How often? Should there be a facilitator, scribe, or timekeeper?

   _____

3. How shall the team solve project/program problems and issues? What tools or techniques will be used?

   _____

4. How will the team make decisions? Will different decisions require different decision-making processes?

   _____

5. Who does what, when, and how in accomplishing team outcomes? What are the specific roles and responsibilities that need to be filled?

   _____

6. How will project effectiveness be judged?

   _____

Operating Guidelines

I D E A

WHAT'S IN IT FOR YOU?

• **Understand how team norms help the team function**

CREATING THE CHARTER

8.10 Team Norms

Despite more than 5,000 years of civilization, when people work together, they still need rules, or norms, on how to deal with each other. A *norm* is an accepted way of doing things. *Team norms* are guiding principles or rules that govern interpersonal conduct among team members. They describe how people should treat each other. If things become unruly, uncomfortable, or dysfunctional, the team norms need to be evoked. Team norms deal with issues such as communication, giving and receiving feedback, leadership, and celebration.

The team needs to make the team norms explicit for the following reasons:

- Certain norms are morale building, and certain norms are not.
- Certain norms lead to high performance, and certain norms do not.
- Certain norms help individuals remain committed to working on the team, and other norms do not
- Implicit norms that are not made explicit may result in conflict, frustration, and unproductive behavior from individual members.
- Explicit norms increase team member satisfaction by reducing ambiguity.
- They increase the potential for interpersonal harmony.
- They decrease the possibility that people will act on their own ideas about what is acceptable. In a diverse group, misunderstandings will abound if people haven't agreed on which behaviors are acceptable and which are not.
- They allow every team member, who so chooses, to be a leader.

Team norms may be ineffective in the following situations:

- Individuals are in competition with each other and use norms to aggravate each other.
- There is no commitment to become a team (such as union management negotiations).
- There are unequal power positions, and no sanction can be used.

Use Ideas 8.11 to 8.13 to help determine your team's agreed-upon and formalized team norms. For more detailed information, see the Ideas listed below:

1. How will the team communicate internally and externally? (See Ideas 13.1–13.11, "Communication.")
2. How will team members give feedback to each other about behavior? (See Ideas 14.1–14.7, "Designated Team Feedback.")
3. How will the issue of leadership be addressed? (See Ideas 15.1–15.4, "Leadership in HITs.")
4. How will the team celebrate together? (See Ideas 20.1–20.4, "Rewards, Recognition, and Celebration.")

Team Norms

IDEA

WHAT'S IN IT FOR YOU?

• **Question the existence and effectiveness of your team's norms**

CREATING THE CHARTER

8.11 Seven Questions About Your Team Norms

As team leader, you need to know the answers to the following questions. If you don't, or if the answers are vague, work with your team members to define team norms. (See Worksheet 8.14.)

1. Have you defined the ways people will behave toward one another?
2. Is there an accepted way of sharing information?
3. How can team members support one another?
4. Is there a method for monitoring team behavior?
5. How will team members evaluate their behaviors from a product perspective and a process perspective?
6. Has the team identified improvement strategies? How will the team handle things that are not getting results? How will the team handle changes within/outside the team?
7. How will individual and team issues of nonperformance be addressed?

Team Norms

I D E A

WHAT'S IN IT FOR YOU?

• **Examine examples of team norms to help in establishing your own**

CREATING THE CHARTER

8.12 Examples of a HIT's Team Norms

1. **Relaxed tone.** The atmosphere of a HIT is informal and comfortable, yet electric and exciting. There are few signs of boredom, and there is a creative tension that comes with people who are challenged, involved, and passionate about their work.

2. **Actively listen.** Team members listen to each other, and people stay on task. In this setting people are not afraid of "trying on" new ideas.

3. **Give honest feedback.** Team members give and take feedback about behaviors they experience in the team's meetings. Criticism is frequent, direct, and given in the spirit of positive regard for others. Feedback is seen as positively seeking to change a team member barrier to a better process.

4. **Express feelings.** Team members understand that passionate commitment to team outcomes will engender strong feelings such as frustration, sadness, anger, delight, and joy. That understanding means team members are free to express feelings as a measure of that commitment.

5. **Make or keep commitments.** Team members make and keep commitments when assignments are accepted. Team members do the work and deliver on the timelines prescribed.

6. **Leadership.** Team leadership shifts over time, depending upon the issue and the team members' expertise. If there is a designated leader, the leader does not dominate, nor does the team defer to the leader. Power is not an issue, but how the outcome is reached is important.

> **Team Norms**

IDEA

- **Learn about team norms that every team should have**

CREATING THE CHARTER

8.13 The Forgotten "Ten" — Norms for Interpersonal Conduct

The following are suggested norms to use, which are sometimes forgotten when teams begin to focus on the work to be produced:

1. **Balance the workload.** Make sure all team members share the load.
2. **Come prepared.** Do the reading and analysis of materials given before the meeting.
3. **Respect your time.** Start on time, stay on time, and end on time. Use the meeting time wisely.
4. **Stay focused.** Don't drift in the meeting — no multi-tasking; be present.
5. **Be open to new ideas.** Listen for what you don't know, and don't prejudge.
6. **Give the benefit of the doubt.** Try not to take comments personally.
7. **Don't talk about team members outside the meetings.** Respect your teammates. Talking behind their backs only fosters discord.
8. **Make and keep commitments.** If you promise to do something, *do it!*
9. **End with process.** Take the last 15 minutes and ask "How was our process?"
10. **Have fun.** Remember to laugh at yourselves.

Team Norms

W O R K S H E E T

WHAT'S IN IT FOR YOU?

• Generate ideas from team members for team norms

CREATING THE CHARTER

8.14 Establishment of Team Norms

Ask each team member to respond to the questions below. Use the worksheets as a reference when the whole team discusses and reaches decisions on team norms.

1. How should team members behave toward one another to create positive working relations?

   _____

2. How will the team effectively share information?

   _____

3. How can team members best support each other?

   _____

4. How will the team evaluate task and process behaviors?

   _____

5. How will the team change things that are not getting results?

   _____

6. How will the team handle changes within/outside the team?

   _____

7. How will team and individual issues of nonperformance be addressed?

   _____

Team Norms

I D E A

• **Help the team determine the roles that need to be established and the people who will fill them**

CREATING THE CHARTER

8.15 Team Responsibilities

Responsibilities are a defined set of roles that the whole team or individual members will be accountable for during the team's operation. There may be (1) collective responsibilities for which the whole team holds one another accountable, (2) paired responsibilities for which two people share accountability, and (3) individual responsibilities for which a person is assigned personal accountability.

It is important to designate responsibilities:

- HITs hold themselves, their teammates, and the whole team responsible for team output.
- Responsibilities prevent a team from being dominated by a leader.
- They keep individuals from being overloaded or uninvolved.
- They allow the team to catch work that otherwise would "fall between the cracks."

| **Responsibility** | = | Collective | + | Paired | + | Individual |

I D E A

• **Understand the nature of collective responsibilities**

CREATING THE CHARTER

8.16 What Is a Collective Responsibility?

Collective responsibilities are held by the entire team, and every member is equally and personally responsible for accomplishing them. Teams in which people feel responsible for their own assignments, but the overall result belongs to the team leader, are not "in tune" with the idea of collective responsibilities. Many collective responsibilities will be found in the outcome statement and team goals. Many, however, will be stated as "norms" that the group will establish later in chartering to help with their team process.

Examples of Collective Responsibilities

- All team members will assist in the resolution of conflict that may occur between two team members.
- The team will design and build a prototype for customer use at 95% accuracy and 99% reliability by X date at a development cost of not more than $500,000.
- All team members will give feedback to each other when appropriate.

Consider the roles and responsibilities that are currently assigned to the entire team membership. Consider which roles and responsibilities are not shared by the collective, but should be.*

Responsibility	=	**Collective**	+	Paired	+	Individual

*See Worksheet 8.24.

IDEA

• **Understand the definition and purpose of paired responsibility**

CREATING THE CHARTER

8.17 What Is Paired Responsibility?

Sharing the responsibility between two (or more) team members is a failsafe measure to ensure the likelihood of an important job, task, or role being done. Paired responsibility is especially wise for parts of the project that are critical to the project's outcomes. When sharing responsibility, one member still has the lead or primary responsibility, and the other team member is given secondary responsibility to monitor and support as needed. Both primary and secondary responsibility holders are fully and equally accountable for the result. Paired responsibility may be a key to creating a team in which peer pressure evolves naturally.

Examples of Paired Responsibility

- Bill will prepare the minutes for the team meetings, and Jan will be the backup to help when asked.
- Susan will head up the market analysis for the prototype, and John will assist as needed.

Consider the roles and responsibilities that are currently shared by two or more people (but not collectively, the entire team). Consider which roles and responsibilities are important enough that they should be shared, but aren't currently.* Be aware as the team progresses that paired responsibilities will be required for some elements of the project.

Responsibility	=	Collective	+	**Paired**	+	Individual

*See Worksheet 8.24.

IDEA

CREATING THE CHARTER

8.18 What Are Individual Responsibilities?

Along with the obligation of team results, an individual team member will be assigned primary responsibility for pieces of work because of his or her particular expertise and interest. The primary responsibility for preparation or fulfillment of the work is individual, but the team will still review and provide input.

Some individual roles will be from the product perspective. These individual responsibilities are related to the team's outcomes and goals:

- Bill will be preparing the minutes of the team meetings for the next six months.
- Bob will be doing a market analysis for this prototype and will present it to the group by X date.
- Jane will examine the software options for this project and will give the team these options for choice by X date.

Other individual roles will be assigned from a process perspective. These individual responsibilities will help the way the team achieves its outcomes and goals:

- Mary will prepare the agendas for the team meetings.
- Harold will make sure the team follows time allocations during meetings.
- Sarah will record decisions on a flip chart.

Consider individuals on your team who currently have designated roles and responsibilities. How were those roles assigned? Are the roles permanent? Are there other individuals who should have a turn at serving a particular role? Do the same members tend to fill important roles over time at the exclusion of others? Are there roles that are not currently filled by individuals, but should be?

| Responsibility | = | Collective | + | Paired | + | **Individual** |

IDEA

• **Assign individual responsibilities for specific process roles**

CREATING THE CHARTER

8.19 Individual Responsibilities — Process Roles

Every team will find it necessary to ask individual team members to fill process roles in order to get work done efficiently. These common process roles help team members adhere to the norms and guidelines agreed upon in the charter.

These roles can be filled by the same person or by different people, depending upon the size, type, and requirements of the group. However, HITs as a rule are not dependent upon one person to fulfill these roles "over the long haul." In fact, one of the hallmarks of HITs is that every group member sees it as his or her responsibility to monitor the team's process and norms as much as possible.

The roles that are typically assigned in HITs:
- Team or meeting leader
- Team process observer
- Team scribe or recorder
- Team member

Answer the following questions:
- Does your team currently have these roles assigned?
- If yes, to whom are they assigned?
- Was it a formal assignment, or did people just drift into the roles?
- Is it time to reevaluate the roles, reassign, or assign them? If yes, the Ideas on the following pages will define the roles in detail.

I D E A

CREATING THE CHARTER

8.20 Process Role — The Team or Meeting Leader*

The function of this role is to lead the team through its work to the outcomes and deliverables agreed upon. In general, the role means to repetitively focus the team on the goals and the processes to achieve those goals. It is also the team leader's role to help team members deal with the interpersonal dynamics that increase their sense of cohesion and honesty.

While initially, team leadership may be assigned or predetermined, in a mature team the team leadership is fluid, constantly changing, always in recognition of skills (technical or human), and above all, shared.

As a team leader, which of the following services do you currently provide? Which services are provided by someone else? Should any of these tasks be assigned or reassigned?

- Helping select team members
- Initiating and facilitating team member changes as needed
- Coordinating and structuring team meetings, including logistics, agendas, minutes, and preparation materials
- Helping the team stick to its espoused process guidelines in the areas of meeting structure, problem solving, decision making, and resolution of conflict
- Ensuring that appropriate data are available or coordinating the processes to explain the data required for problem analysis and solution
- Acting as the hub for subgroup sharing of information
- Coordinating the interface between the team and other outside individuals and groups
- Clarifying and summarizing team decisions and action plans
- Ensuring that every team member has a chance to participate.

*See "Leadership in HITs," Ideas 15.1–15.4, for a more elaborate discussion of this topic.

I D E A

• Understand the definition and services of the role of the process observer

CREATING THE CHARTER

8.21 Process Role — The Process Observer

The function of a process observer or facilitator is to aid the team in both its interpersonal dynamics and its group processes. This role helps the team maintain high levels of synergy in problem solving. The process observer role will also help prevent behaviors motivated by self-interest that may affect team decision making and conflict resolution.

The person in this role must be vigilant about observing team members' behavior and holding them accountable to follow the processes they agreed to.

The process observer's role includes the following tasks:

- Continually reminding team members of appropriate team and interpersonal behaviors
- Aiding the team in sticking to its espoused problem-solving process
- Reminding the team of its commitment to its operating guidelines
- Initiating and supporting feedback to team members and the team about their behavior
- Making suggestions about how people can improve their individual and collective performance
- Helping the team reach consensus
- Helping individuals resolve conflict and deal with disagreement without long-term damage to interpersonal relationships
- Making the team aware of its use of time
- Asking questions or clarifying statements.

The process observer role may be a permanently assigned role, but it may be more effective to rotate it periodically. Who currently fills this function on your team? Is this a role that needs to be assigned or reassigned?

I D E A

CREATING THE CHARTER

8.22 Process Role — The Team Scribe or Recorder

The function of this role is to record, in writing, the major themes expressed in meetings. Typically, the team scribe has the responsibility to track team discussion during the meetings, as well as handle the logistics of minutes, agendas, and materials needed by team members. This team member is also a fully participating member.

Specific activities may include the following tasks:

- Capturing major themes of team discussions
- Recording major action items and decisions made by the team
- Publishing the action plans, minutes, and assignments within the time frames defined by the team
- Serving as the focal point for agenda items that team members want included, setting the agenda, and establishing timelines for the next meeting
- Serving as an active member of the team by contributing ideas, advocating a position, etc., within the team guidelines and norms.

Because of the detailed nature of this role, it is better to have one individual fill the role, reassigning only periodically. How are the specific tasks of the scribe currently being done? Is there a need for an assignment or reassignment of this role?

IDEA

WHAT'S IN IT FOR YOU?

- **Understand the definition and services of the team member**

CREATING THE CHARTER

8.23 Process Role — The Team Member

Why bother to define the team member role? Isn't it obvious? Don't count on it. Most Westerners don't have the cultural understanding of what it means to be an effective team member.*

It is necessary to specify the expectations you have for people both during and in between team meetings. The role of team member requires commitment to both the task at hand and interpersonal relationships.

Specific expectations for the team member include the following:
- Participates actively, attends all meetings, and contributes honestly
- Accepts and completes all assignments given
- Shows commitment to team outcomes and process by demonstrating the appropriate behaviors
- Adheres to a problem-solving process agreed to by the team
- Supports the chosen decision-making process by acting in accordance with the decisions after a full discussion
- Subordinates personal goals and agendas with the understanding that team goals are more important
- Stays flexible and open to new ideas and alternatives that aid the team in reaching its outcomes
- Acts as a process observer who helps the team self-correct when the team is not following its espoused guidelines
- Respects the confidentiality of team members and of team topics of discussion.

Take stock of your team members. Do you believe they understand and agree with what the role of a team member is? Clarifying team operating guidelines in Ideas 8.6–8.8 and team norms in Ideas 8.10–8.13 will help team members focus on the attitudes and behaviors that build HITs.

---

*In a worldwide study of 116,000 employees of IBM, Dutch psychologist Geert Hofstede was able to rank 40 cultures according to the strength of individualism or collectivism. The five most strongly individualistic cultures were in the United States, Australia, Great Britain, Canada, and the Netherlands, in that order. This study was cited as just one example of how Westerners' individualistic culture makes it difficult to work in teams and accept the group's goals as superceding individual goals. [Daniel Goleman, "Individualism vs Eastern Cultures," *The Straights Times* (January 28, 1991).]

W O R K S H E E T

WHAT'S IN IT FOR YOU?

• Identify the team's responsibilities from a process perspective

CREATING THE CHARTER

8.24 Responsibilities, Shared and Individual

Once the operating guidelines and team norms are established, identify which roles and responsibilities are collective, which are paired, and which are individual. This distinction is important to ensure balance between a team approach and individual accountability. This worksheet gives you an opportunity to clarify existing roles and evaluate assignments or reassignments that need to be made.

Collective Responsibilities
(Clear statements of responsibilities to be shared by every team member)

_____

_____

_____

_____

_____

Paired Responsibilities
(Clear statements of responsibilities to be shared by two team members, one acting as a support to the other)_____

_____

_____

_____

_____

Individual Responsibilities
(Clear statements of responsibilities for which an individual will be held accountable)

_____

_____

_____

_____

_____

IDEA

- **Understand the charter endorsement and how it signals the true beginning of the team's work**

CREATING THE CHARTER

8.25 The Charter Endorsement

The charter endorsement is the final step in the chartering process. Ideally, agreement on the charter's specifics should be completed by the team leader and team, then the sponsor, before the team starts its work. Then finally, the charter should be shared with the organization at large.

Charter endorsement is often neglected in the chartering process, but it is important for some fairly obvious reasons:

- Charter endorsement is the signal to the team for the beginning of formal accountability for project outcomes.
- The team's endorsement is a statement of agreement to commit to the members' best efforts.
- The team sponsor's endorsement means that the team has the authority to carry out its charter.
- The organization-at-large should see the charter endorsement as the formal beginning of the team's work.

There are three steps in the charter endorsement for you to consider. If you determine that your team does not have a formally endorsed charter, refer to Ideas 5.1–5.15, "Initiating the Charter."

Charter Endorsement	=	Team Endorsement	+	Sponsor Endorsement	+	Communication to Others

WORKSHEET

WHAT'S IN IT FOR YOU?

- Ascertain a team member's level of agreement with the charter by understanding team endorsement and the types of questions to pose

CREATING THE CHARTER

8.26 Stepping Up or Stepping Off: The Team's Charter Endorsement

The team must understand and approve the scope of work it's committing to take on before presenting the charter to the sponsor for endorsement and to the community at large. All team members must fully and completely agree to work toward endorsement of the charter — working out any individual reservations about various components.

The following questions will help you and your team members assess the level of commitment or prospective problems each individual has with the charter.

- Do you think the charter represents the group's best thinking? If no, why not?
- Will the charter require you to behave in ways that are against your personal values? If yes, how? Is this a serious issue that will affect your contribution to the team? Do you see any way to solve the issue?
- Is it important for you to object to the charter? Why?
- If you have reservations, are they based on sound fact? Do you believe the team has fully heard your reservations? Do you feel you have had an opportunity to influence the team? (If the answer is no, help the team member's ideas be heard and understood, if not accepted.)
- If you have reservations, are they strong enough that you may choose not to give your best effort?

The team must be unified around a common purpose, outcomes, guidelines, and norms. Each team member must agree to commit his or her best efforts to the team outcomes. Team members, having had their chance to influence the charter, must now fully agree to support the charter or be prepared to step out of the team.

Charter Endorsement	=	**Team Endorsement**	+	Sponsor Endorsement	+	Communication to Others

I D E A

• **Help the team determine how to obtain sponsor agreement to the charter**

CREATING THE CHARTER

8.27 Getting the Go-Ahead: Sponsor Endorsement

The charter should be endorsed in person or in writing by the team sponsor or, if no sponsor has been designated, by the individual or group to whom the team reports. If the management has appointed a sponsor, then both should endorse the charter. If management has formed the team and appointed a sponsor for liaison and support, the endorsement should come from the manager or managers who have appointed the team.

The sponsor's and/or managerial endorsement means approval is given for the content of the charter and the commitment to support it with resources as required.

The following questions will help you and the sponsor and/or management to verify the endorsement:

- Is there any part of the charter that needs to be elaborated on, for further understanding?
- Are the outcomes and deliverables seen as beneficial to the organization?
- Are any processes or outcomes against organizational values?
- How will the team, sponsor, and/or management team communicate frequently enough to meet the needs of all concerned?
- What behaviors does the team want from the sponsor and/or management as an indicator of support?

Charter Endorsement	=	Team Endorsement	+	**Sponsor Endorsement**	+	Communication to Others

I D E A

WHAT'S IN IT FOR YOU?

- **Help the team determine how to communicate the charter to the rest of the organization**

CREATING THE CHARTER

8.28 Communicating with the Organizational Community

Once the charter has been endorsed by the team members, the sponsor, and/or management, it should be shared with those groups and individuals with whom the team will work most. Of course, it is prudent to communicate some general information to the organizational community-at-large.

By sharing the team's charter with individuals and groups of primary contacts, the team can increase its credibility and probability of success with these external groups.

Finally, the endorsement process should be completed by announcing the team's purpose, outcomes, and timelines to the general organizational community. By doing so, the team announces a formal accountability for its work and stakes out its "territory" to the rest of the organization.

The following questions will help you ask the team how to share the charter with the organizational community:

- What information would be of interest to the groups with whom the team will have the most contact? To the organization-at-large?
- What is the most appropriate means of communicating the charter to the organization-at-large? E-mail, Intranet, organizational newsletter, bulletin-board posting, memo?
- How can the team produce periodic updates on a routine basis that can be done easily and efficiently?
- What information should not be shared at this time?
- What "image" does the team want to present to the organizational community?

Charter Endorsement	=	Team Endorsement	+	Sponsor Endorsement	+	**Communication to Others**

SECTION 2

DEVELOPING IDEAS: HELPING TEAMS OPERATE MORE EFFECTIVELY

High Impact Teams obviously do things better than most other groups. The difference is in the way they go about their work! While the technology and resources may not differ greatly, HITs are better at maintaining a process perspective than nonperforming teams. HITs realize that it is natural to focus on the product perspective — that's how the team will be judged by the outside world — but without the process perspective, they may never achieve their goals.

Visualize product and process discussions in a group in the following way

TEAM INTERACTIONS

Product Discussions	**Process Discussions**
• What are the desired products?	• How will issues be decided?
• What actions will be taken?	• How can problem solving be done?
• How will the product make a difference?	• How should members treat each other?

The process perspective can be further subdivided into

1. Operating guidelines or procedures that are concerned with team output (i.e., meeting structure, problem solving, decision making, conflict resolution)
2. Norms or rules concerned with interpersonal conduct (i.e., communication, feedback, leadership, reward).

TEAM INTERACTIONS

Product Discussions	**Process Discussions**

• Operating guidelines or procedures — team output

• Norms or rules — interpersonal conduct

DEVELOPING IDEAS: THE MINIMUM EIGHT

If you are forming a team and are deciding around which areas you should form guidelines and norms, consider at a minimum the following eight areas:

Guidelines:

- **Meeting structure.** The team's use of agendas, minutes, and meeting logs
- **Problem solving.** The steps of defining the problem, generating alternatives, analyzing, making choices, implementing solutions, and evaluating
- **Decision making.** The choices of consensus, majority rule, minority rule, leader decides, and "no decision"
- **Conflict resolution.** The strategies of accepting, retreating, contesting, modifying, and creating

Norms:

- **Communication.** The use of attending behavior, summarizing, paraphrasing, questioning, and reflecting feelings
- **Feedback.** The skills of giving and receiving information concerning interpersonal behavior
- **Leadership.** The sharing of power
- **Rewards.** The rewarding and recognizing of team members.

The first eight topics are addressed in this Section, Chapters 9–17, along with suggestions for team training and assessing team process. The eighth norm, (rewards), is explored in more depth in Section 3, Chapter 20.

CHAPTER NINE

MEETING STRUCTURE

WHAT'S IN IT FOR YOU?

- Identify which of the five types of meetings your team requires
- Ensure more effective meetings by following six steps in planning, conducting, and following up meetings
- Calculate the costs of having a meeting and weight the cost/benefit
- Build agendas that stimulate rather than hinder productivity
- Evaluate the effectiveness of your meetings

Meetings are how teams do their work. They are also expensive. They can also be gigantic time wasters. It makes sense that the time and effort be taken to establish practices that are consistent and helpful — pre-meeting, during, and post-meeting. This chapter not only outlines ideas for structuring your meetings, it also provides worksheets and samples of agendas, minutes, and logs.

I D E A

MEETING STRUCTURE

9.1 Isn't a Structure Confining?

Does your team have a meeting structure it can depend on to get the work done efficiently? Meeting structure is actually a set of operating guidelines that establish an accepted way for team members to bring up, schedule, and clarify task-related issues in order for the team to do its work. Meeting structure is created through agendas, minutes, and meeting logs. Despite what might feel like added work, meeting structure benefits the team in very important ways:

- It orders the flow of team discussion.
- It allows for documentation of work accomplished.
- It helps to orient new team members.
- It helps team members prepare to contribute to team meetings.
- It helps teams create their own history and language.

Meeting structure can be ineffective

- in R&D teams that have no clear purpose
- in therapeutic groups or teams concerned with personal issues
- in informal teams that meet once or twice for the main purpose of information sharing
- when the structure doesn't support the type and purpose of the meeting.

You know your meeting structure is effective when it promotes the purpose of the meeting with efficiency and inclusion, but not at the expense of creativity and informality.

IDEA

- **Identify the types of meetings your team requires**

MEETING STRUCTURE

9.2 Five Purposes of Team Meetings

Meetings can be the bane of a team's existence. Meetings are also the lifeblood of a team and the way a team goes about doing what it does. Shared or common experience and participation are two hallmarks of a sense of community necessary for creating HITs. Even though your team will be meeting for a variety of the reasons listed below, it is important to create a meeting structure that begins to build a common approach to working together and creating a team history and language.

Every meeting should have a purpose. The following are five principal reasons for meetings:

- **Define the team.** Meetings can be held simply to help everyone become better team members. The meeting can be used to introduce people, establish rules, assign responsibilities, build commitment, or establish schedules for future events.
- **Share information.** A meeting is the most efficient means of ensuring that all team members have access to the same information. Questions can be answered and clarification provided. A meeting can give a common base of knowledge from which a sense of mutual responsibility can begin.
- **Generate ideas and set outcomes.** The positive potential of a group lies in its possible synergy. The combination of all team members' ideas becomes the ground from which new ideas spring. Teams with synergy tend to have outcomes of higher quality, take better risks, and have fewer errors.
- **Assign work responsibilities.** The meeting provides a forum for allotting responsibilities and tasks based upon skills and commitment. Meetings create an opportunity for greater efficiency and workload balance.
- **Review project progress.** Meetings can be used to judge progress being made on the project and start to make modifications if the project is not on target. Meetings are also a time to review individual performance related to group goals.

I D E A

• **Learn six steps to improve the effectiveness of your meetings**

MEETING STRUCTURE

9.3 Six Steps to More Effective Meetings

No matter what the purpose of your meeting is, the following six steps will create a meeting structure that helps the team work more effectively.

1. Plan
   • The objectives of the meeting
   • The agenda of topics / issues to be covered
   • Participants or meeting membership

2. Disseminate the Agenda
   • Include the purpose for meeting, topics, and related information
   • Include individual, paired, or collective responsibilities and expectations that require preparation

3. Prepare
   • Sequence the agenda items
   • Assign time based on importance, not urgency
   • Arrange for room setup and amenities
   • Prepare materials

4. Conduct
   • Present and discuss issues, topics, and evidence
   • Interpret facts
   • Reach conclusions and make decisions
   • List actions to take
   • Don't jump ahead, rehash old ground, or jump to different topics

5. Summarize
   • Summarize and record decisions
   • Designate person(s) responsible for action follow-up

6. Follow up
   • Send minutes of the meeting to each team member
   • Send a written summary of action steps and expectations as a result of meeting

I D E A

- **Assess the costs of your team meetings**

MEETING STRUCTURE

9.4 The Cost of a Meeting

If you knew how much a team meeting costs, you might think twice about the way the meeting is structured. If you examine the cost of one meeting that could be multiplied by a number of meetings over time, you may find teams are costly. We're not advocating reduction of meetings necessarily, but the more efficient use of the time you spend together.

Steps for Determining the Cost of a Meeting

1. Estimate the total annual salaries for all people in the meeting.
    - For example, $224,000 for 7 people ($32,000 yearly salary x 7 people)
2. Divide the total salary amount by 243 days (365 days minus 52 weekends = 261 days minus 3 days Thanksgiving, 5 days Christmas, and 10 days vacation = 243)
    - $224,000 divided by 243 days = $922 per day
3. Divide the day rate for the group of $922 by 8 hours to estimate hourly rate for the group.
    - $922 per day divided by 8 = $115 per hour
4. Multiply the hourly rate for the group by the number of hours met.
    - $115 per hour x 3 hours = $345.

Examples

- A group of 7 people with a collective annual salary of $224,000 who meet for 3 hours will cost the organization $345.
- A group of 7 people with collective annual salaries of $434,000 ($62,000 per year) meeting for 3 hours will cost the organization $669.

These estimates do not include facilities costs, food costs, equipment costs, manpower costs for those coordinating the meeting who do not attend, outside resources costs, team member travel expenses, or loss of productivity costs because team members are attending the meeting and not doing their regular jobs.

Make your team meetings count!

I D E A

MEETING STRUCTURE

9.5 Capturing History

The danger in oral communication is believing it's been understood and agreed upon. By recording and making the flow of the team's discussion visible *as it happens*, you help ensure that team members are sharing the same meaning and conclusions as the discussion progresses.

As the conversation is actually occurring, write down or type the main ideas that the team is dealing with and make them visible. You do not have to record the discussion word for word as a court recorder might produce a transcript, but the main ideas, questions, issues, suggestions, or feelings should be recorded.

Recording the conversation visually can be done as follows:

- Have someone scribe or record the discussion on chart paper.
- Use Power Point, which is prominently displayed on a screen that all members can see.
- Do a "mind-mapping" diagram on a white board, flip chart, blackboard, or other large surface.

"Public scribing" creates a team reality that allows everyone to focus on the issues, understand them, and contribute. The recording then becomes the basis for minutes and future agendas.

IDEA

• **Understand the individual and shared roles during team meetings**

MEETING STRUCTURE

9.6 Roles in a Meeting

The roles listed below are not to be considered the sole responsibility of one person. In fact, HITs expect team members to assume the behaviors under the listed roles whenever the need arises. While these behaviors are assigned to the roles, they are not to be seen as exclusive to the roles.

Team Leader/Facilitator

- Convenes the group and ensures that all preparations are in order
- Clarifies the objectives of the meeting
- Clarifies the decision-making process to be used and monitors its implementation
- Ensures that the meeting stays focused and attention is given to both task and process issues
- Monitors task leadership and ensures that those with the most expertise will exercise leadership appropriately
- Summarizes the action plan
- Ensures fellowship

Recorder/Scribe

- Records attendance
- Lists topics as discussed
- Summarizes notes
- Distributes minutes

Participants

- Participate according to the rules established by the team
- Provide task-related input on topics
- Speak honestly about feelings
- Implement mutually agreed-upon assignments after the meeting

I D E A

MEETING STRUCTURE

9.7 An Agenda for Agendas

Agendas often fall into the category of bureaucratic paperwork — a list of things for people to ignore. A properly prepared agenda, however, is a critical part of a HIT team meeting:

- An agenda allows team members to anticipate and be prepared for team discussions.
- It allows people to shape the meeting as it proceeds.
- It allows team members to stay on track.
- It allows topics to be accessed when reviewing team progress.
- It allows team members to shape future meetings.

The only negatives to an agenda are that a bad one can thwart a team's creativity and work flow, and any agenda can be subpoenaed in court proceedings.

Consider these "givens" when creating your next agenda:

- Agenda items are not decided if interested team members are not present.
- Agenda items, as a rule, should not be established if no preparation has been done.
- Items added in the meeting, as a rule, should have backup reading material distributed by the sponsoring team members (preferably before the meeting).
- Agendas should not be used as an excuse or rationale to forego quality discussions.
- Adequate thought should be given to the selection and inclusion of agenda items in order for quality decisions to be made by all team members.
- Agendas should be distributed prior to the meeting with enough time given for people to prepare themselves adequately.
- The agenda should be agreed upon as the meeting starts to thwart any hidden agendas or to accommodate changes when necessary.

I D E A

• **Learn tips for creating an effective agenda**

MEETING STRUCTURE

9.8 Ten Considerations for Your Meeting Agenda

1. Allow 48 business hours for any team member to add relevant business issues to the agenda
2. Close the agenda 24 hours before the meeting.
3. Distribute the agenda to team members at least 24 hours before the meeting (more if longer preparation time is required).
4. Assign the preparation of the agenda to one group member to create a sense of continuity.
5. Discuss and agree upon criteria for what are appropriate agenda items (for example, Is the topic strategic vs. tactical? Does the issue involve two or more team members?).
6. Assign a tentative timeline to each agenda item.
7. Designate the name of the team member who requested the issue be put on the agenda.
8. Ask the team member who put the issue on the agenda to "frame" the issue, problem, or topic on paper to be included with or in the agenda.
9. Ask the team member who put the issue on the agenda to include pertinent background material, data, or information to be read before the meeting.
10. Start the meeting by asking team members if there are any "emergency" items that should be added.

I D E A

- **Learn how to label agenda items for maximum efficiency**

MEETING STRUCTURE

9.9 Organizing Your Meeting Agenda

When you label your agenda items as information items, discussion items, or decision items,* you can attribute adequate time frames to topics and help people come prepared to do what needs to be done at the meeting.

Information Items

- Information items are issues about which the team members need to be informed. Usually, these items are updates on recent developments — for example, subcommittee progress — that are relevant to team members.
- Information items should be written, circulated with the agenda, and read by team members prior to the meeting.
- Information items should take very little time for discussion.
- Information items should be commented on for clarification only.

Discussion Items

- Discussion items should be worded by the sponsoring team member as a question (e.g., Should the team spend X$ for ABC equipment? Should the team formulate a policy on … ?).
- Discussion items imply that no decision will be reached the first time they appear on the agenda as discussion items.
- Discussion items can appear on the agenda as decision items for the next team meeting, but they can also be listed as discussion items until the issue is fully explored.
- Discussion items are just that — discussion items. The issue should be examined from all possible angles. The pros and cons of alternative solutions should be aired.
- Discussion items should be allotted the most amount of time on the agenda. In a three-hour meeting, it is not unusual to spend 20 to 40 minutes or more on one discussion item.

- Discussion items should be brainstormed. Using a disciplined brainstorming technique,** all possible alternatives should be generated, and the pros and cons for each alternative should be fully explored.
- Discussion items should be concluded by a designation of
  a. To be decided at the next meeting
  b. Discussion item in the next meeting
  c. Drop from further discussion.

Decision Items

- Decision items should be worded as a decision statement (e.g., The team will/will not spend X\$ for ABC equipment by X date. The team will/will not formulate a policy on ABC by X date).
- Decision items for which a consensus or decision cannot be reached during the time allotted would be labeled as decision items for the next meeting.
- Decision items that cannot reach resolution a second time should be labeled as discussion items for the next meeting.
- Decision items should take little time on the agenda, perhaps 15 minutes to review past discussions, before a decision is reached.

---

*These are guidelines that could be modified depending upon the type of organizational culture.

**See "Problem Solving," Ideas 10.12–10.13, for information on brainstorming techniques.

I D E A

• **Learn how to include team members in building and planning an agenda**

MEETING STRUCTURE

9.10 Eliminating Hidden Agendas

By including team members in the creation and approval of the agenda prior to the meeting, you are flushing out hidden agendas. When you give people a chance to voice their needs and have team members agree or disagree, the agenda becomes a team effort, rather than an opportunity for a potentially manipulative individual agenda. Use these ideas to include team members in building the agenda:

- Review minutes from the last meeting for accuracy before the agenda is discussed.
- Ask team members to prioritize the agenda items according to
  — importance to group members
  — importance to those outside the team
  — importance to the sequence of future work
  — additional information required for adequate discussion
  — the absence of key team members
  — team timelines.
- Ask team members to discuss and approve the allotted times given for each agenda item.
- Ask team members to check the appropriateness of discussion and decision items.
- At end of each meeting, ask team members for potential topics for the next meeting.

WORKSHEET

WHAT'S IN IT FOR YOU?

- **Use this suggested agenda topics worksheet to solicit agenda items from team members**

MEETING STRUCTURE

9.11 Suggested Agenda Topics Worksheet

SUGGESTED AGENDA TOPICS

Team Member Name: _____   Team Name: _____

Date of Meeting: _____   Location:_____

Information item(s)	**Priority**	**Time allotment**
Should be read by team members prior to; take very little time; comments for clarification only	1 2 3 4 5	☐ Attach handouts
_____	_____	_____ Mins.
_____	_____	_____ Mins.
_____	_____	_____ Mins.
_____	_____	_____ Mins.

Discussion item(s)		
Phrased as a question; no decision will be reached; elevated to decision item for next meeting		
_____	_____	_____ Mins.
_____	_____	_____ Mins.
_____	_____	_____ Mins.
_____	_____	_____ Mins.

Decision item(s)		
Should be worded as a decision; take little time on the agenda		
_____	_____	_____ Mins.
_____	_____	_____ Mins.
_____	_____	_____ Mins.
_____	_____	_____ Mins.

Please forward to: _____   by:_____

Phone: _____   Fax:_____

W O R K S H E E T

WHAT'S IN IT FOR YOU?

- **Examine a sample agenda format to use at your next meeting**

MEETING STRUCTURE

9.12 Agenda Format Example

Name of team or committee: Cross-Functional Marketing Team
Date: 3/22/98
Time: 9:00 a.m.
Location: R306

Purpose(s) of the meeting: ❑ Define the team   ❑ Share information
❑ Generate ideas and outcomes   ❑ Assign work responsibilities
❑ Review program progress

Facilitator: Bob N.
Process observer: Josie K.
Scribe: Roger L.
Timekeeper: Sandra M.

Attendees: Mark, Sharon, Nancy, Bob, Roger, Sandra, Josie, Robin
Please read: Minutes of 3/18; attached updates
Please bring: Updates and personal calendars

Agenda Topics

1. Information item _____Who _____Time _____
2. Information item _____Who _____Time _____
3. Information item _____Who _____Time _____
4. Discussion item _____Who _____Time _____
5. Discussion item _____Who _____Time _____
6. Discussion item _____Who _____Time _____
7. Decision item _____Who _____Time _____
8. Decision item _____Who _____Time _____
9. Decision item _____Who _____Time _____
10. Process meeting_____Who _____Time _____

Other information:

Special notes:

I D E A

- **Examine the reasons why minutes are important**

MEETING STRUCTURE

9.13 Meetings: Minute by Minute

Minutes have been much maligned, and perhaps rightly so. They serve an important purpose, but the formality and work make them seem redundant and bureaucratic. Lest you forget why minutes serve a vital function, consider the following reasons for documenting your team meeting:

- Documentation of a meeting allows team members to review what has been discussed or decided.
- It helps team members prepare for subsequent meetings.
- It gives team members a sense of task movement or accomplishment.
- It allows for the expedient introduction of new members.
- It tends to cut down on repetitive discussions.
- If the minutes aren't worth taking and reading, maybe the meeting wasn't worth having.

Are there any reasons not to have minutes? Minutes may not be necessary if the team has limited resources. Because the minutes can be subpoenaed in court proceedings, you may not want to record minutes if the topics or issues are particularly sensitive or subject to litigation.

There are "givens" for you to consider when preparing minutes:

- All team opinions, ideas, or suggestions should be included in the minutes, although team member names are not necessary.
- A team member can be assigned the responsibility of scribe, or the responsibility can be rotated from team member to team member. Assignment should be made before the meeting starts.
- A standard format for minutes should be used and followed by all team members responsible for the minutes.
- Minutes should be reviewed by all team members for accuracy. This review should be the first agenda item for the subsequent meeting.

W O R K S H E E T

WHAT'S IN IT FOR YOU?

• **Examine a sample format to use for organizing the minutes of your meetings**

MEETING STRUCTURE

9.14   Sample Format for Minutes

If people are not reading the minutes of your meetings, it may be because they are not relevant, easy to read, or helpful. Consider the following format for preparing minutes that people will actually read.

Title of committee or team:
Date held:
Time held:
Location:

Type of meeting:
Facilitator:
Scribe:
Process observer:
Attendees:

Agenda Topics

Topic_____ Who _____ Time _____

Discussion:

Conclusion:

Action Items_____ Deadline _____

Person Responsible_____

Discussion:

Conclusion:

W O R K S H E E T

WHAT'S IN IT FOR YOU?

• Track what occurs in your team meetings

MEETING STRUCTURE

9.15 Meeting Log Worksheet

Use this format to track and record what occurs during your team meetings.

Purpose of the meeting:

Attendees:

Date _____ **Start** _____ **End** _____

Agenda Item & Action(s) Needed	Time Allotted	Who	Review Date	Deadline
1. Item_____ Action _____				
2. Item_____ Action _____				
3. Item_____ Action _____				
4. Item_____ Action _____				
5. Item_____ Action _____				
6. Item_____ Action _____				
7. Item_____ Action _____				

Next Meeting: _____ **Time:** _____ **Place:** _____

W O R K S H E E T

WHAT'S IN IT FOR YOU?

• Complete a checklist to assure that you plan your meeting effectively

MEETING STRUCTURE

9.16 Meeting Evaluation Checklist

	Yes	No
1. Seating in the room was arranged so everyone could see everyone else.	❏	❏
2. Equipment was provided to record ideas and decisions.	❏	❏
3. Agenda was presented, amended, and/or agreed upon.	❏	❏
4. Time estimates were determined for each item.	❏	❏
5. At least once or twice during the meeting someone asked "Is everyone satisfied with the team process? How can we be more productive?"	❏	❏
6. Ideas generated and decisions made during the meeting were recorded, prepared, and distributed to team members some time later.	❏	❏
7. The meeting records designated who agreed to do what and by when.	❏	❏
8. Dates for future meetings were set well in advance so arrangements could be made by team members to attend.	❏	❏
9. Those in attendance considered whether others should be involved in future meetings or decisions and if so, who.	❏	❏
10. At the end of the meeting, team members took some time to discuss what worked and how future meetings might be improved.	❏	❏

CHAPTER 10

PROBLEM SOLVING

WHAT'S IN IT FOR YOU?

- Learn why solving problems from a team perspective is more effective than individual problem solving
- Create the conditions that support team problem solving
- Follow a six-step problem-solving model
- Refer to additional resources to enhance learning

Problems, problems, … you just knew there'd be problems. Better to count on problems and be ready to solve them, than ignore them and have them potentially destroy your team. This chapter provides a step-by-step process for going beyond problem spotting to problem solving through clearly identifying the problem, then generating, examining, and choosing alternatives.

I D E A

WHAT'S IN IT FOR YOU?

• **Understand why HITs follow a process for problem solving**
• **Understand what can block effective problem solving**

PROBLEM SOLVING

10.1 Moving from Problem Spotters to Problem Solvers

Problem solving is a set of steps that all team members follow to reach the best possible solution for the team's work. When a sound problem-solving process is used, the solution formed by the team is often far more effective than single solutions proposed by individuals because there is a better chance that all members have bought into the solution.

A problem-solving process, when used correctly by a team, can

- allow all team members to contribute their ideas.
- lead to a full and comprehensive examination of the issue.
- result in the generation of untapped alternatives.
- help team members assess the pros and cons of alternatives.
- allow team members to support an organized process in which they are committed to finding the best solution, rather than accepting an exclusive view.
- legitimize conflict and challenge in order to test ideas and their usefulness in reaching a solution.

Problem solving is ineffective when the following conditions exist:

- Team members are not technically competent.
- Leaders overrule the group.
- All points of view are not drawn out or considered.
- Team members fear conflict more than a poor decision.
- Inaccurate or incomplete data are used.

IDEA

- **Learn what a team leader needs to do to help support a team approach to problem solving**

PROBLEM SOLVING

10.2 Ten Conditions That Support Team Problem Solving

As a team leader, ask yourself what you can do to foster the conditions listed below. Some of them may require a change in your own belief about your role as a team leader. It is your job to teach the team members how to solve their own problems — not to solve the problems for them. Remember that ultimately your success as a team leader lies in the success of your team, not in exercising your ego. HITs become HITs because they know how to find solutions as a team.

Ten Conditions That Support Team Problem Solving

1. The team leader participates as a team member and is subject to the same rules.
2. Team decisions are not arbitrarily overruled by the leader simply because the leader does not agree with them.
3. Conflict arising from different points of view is thought of as helpful and is resolved constructively by the team.
4. Team members challenge suggestions they believe are not founded on facts or logic, but they avoid arguing just to have their way.
5. Poor solutions or alternatives are not supported for the sake of peace and harmony.
6. Differences of opinion are explored and resolved; consensus is reached rather than voting on or avoiding the issues.
7. Each member works to make the problem-solving process as effective as possible and tries to facilitate rather than hinder discussion.
8. Each team member understands the value of time and works to eliminate extraneous or repetitious discussion.
9. Team members encourage and support fellow team members who may be reticent to offer their ideas or suggestions.
10. The problem worked on by the team requires multiple viewpoints and technological collaboration.

I D E A

• **Develop a model to help your team mutually solve problems**

PROBLEM SOLVING

10.3 A Standard Six-Step Problem-Solving Model

A group that does not follow a problem-solving model may not only get poor results, but could also end up solving the wrong problem. A problem-solving model provides team members with clear, simple (although perhaps not easy) guidelines for working together to find a solution they can all support.

There are myriad problem-solving models to chose from,* but they all seem to have these six basic steps in common:

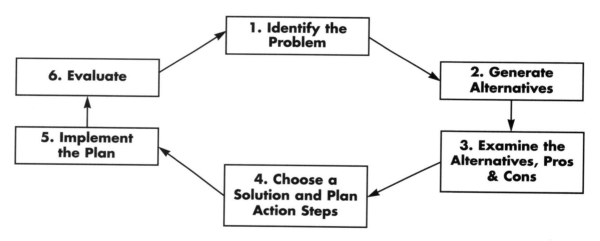

Some basic rules apply to the effectiveness of the problem-solving model:
- All six steps are important for achieving the best results.
- Each step should be taken one at a time by the group and in the correct order.
- The problem should be fully defined and understood by team members before solutions are discussed.
- Try to avoid discussing a solution before the alternatives have been fully generated.

The Ideas that follow define the six steps and explain how to achieve them in more detail.

---

*See Idea 10.17 for a list of resources.

I D E A

WHAT'S IN IT FOR YOU?

• **Understand why taking time to identify the true problem is an investment of time**

PROBLEM SOLVING

10.4 The First Step: Identifying the Problem

The first step of identifying the problem seems obvious, but usually, people see only part of a problem, or they see only the symptoms. It is normal for a team to mistake a symptom or one person's view for "the problem."

Looking beyond the symptom really must be done as a team. Problem identification necessitates the help of many people who view the issue from different perspectives. The real problem or issue is identified when many viewpoints are merged and synthesized.

Consider the following when identifying the "real" problem that needs solving:

- Take your time! Depending upon your team's size, the type of team, and the capacity of team members to work together, problem identification may take a while.
- It is important to be precise because precision clarifies the group's work, enhances team member commitment, and aids the conservation of resources needed for implementation.
- In identifying the problem, be careful not to "choose" a problem simply because the solution or resources are readily available.
- Create a problem statement that succinctly clarifies the problem that needs to be solved.

W O R K S H E E T

PROBLEM SOLVING

10.5 Worksheet for Identifying the Problem

Ask team members these questions to help identify the problem:

1. Why is the problem a problem?

2. What happens because of the problem?

3. Who is affected by the problem and how?

4. What are the consequences?

5. What are the causes of the problem?

6. Why does the problem exist?

7. Does it result from the way the organization is set up?

8. Does it result from the way one or more people do things?

9. Does it happen because people lack information?

10. Does it happen because people expect things that are not possible?

11. Does it happen because people have different goals?

I D E A

PROBLEM SOLVING

10.6 Identifying the Problem — The Affinity Diagram

Making an Affinity Diagram is a technique used to amass large numbers of ideas, opinions, and data; sort them into categories based on their affinity or relationship; and name them for easier analysis and work allocation.

This procedure is similar to brainstorming because there is a premium placed upon the creation of many ideas. Then, these ideas are sorted into groupings, which give insight into the issue or problem that needs solving.

In this technique the quantity of ideas is emphasized over the quality of ideas; therefore, there is no weighting or prioritizing of the ideas.

An Affinity Diagram is most beneficial when

- facts or thoughts are in chaos
- issues are too large or complex
- a breakthrough in traditional thinking is needed
- support for an alternative is essential
- potential causes of a problem need to be organized.

An Affinity Diagram might be ineffective when little time is available to gather data, or when very little is known about the problem or issue.

I D E A

PROBLEM SOLVING

10.7 Identifying the Problem — How to Complete an Affinity Diagram

STEP 1. STATE THE TOPIC

State the topic to be discussed. The main reason for the selection of the topic is that it contains many of the issues that concern the team members. Most people will have some relevant information to bring to the discussion.

Example: *What are the reasons we are missing shipping dates?*

STEP 2. GENERATE AND LIST IDEAS

The second step is to generate ideas that help team members understand the issue and why it exists. These single ideas should be recorded on 3 x 5 cards or self-adhesive notes where they can be seen and reached by all team members.

Warehouse inventory not current	High turnover of warehouse staff	Labels fall off boxes	Bonus system rewards speed
Products not properly labeled on shelves	Insufficient lead time given by sales	Lack of training of order entry people	Order entry too complex
Product damaged in shipping	Computer system needs updating	This is peak time of year	A lot of new employees in shipping
Customer order forms have wrong information	Use lowest price carrier	Zip codes are changing	Pricing changed but not in computer

STEP 3. GROUP THE IDEAS

At this point, team members should arrange the cards or self-adhesive notes into related groups *without discussion*. The silence is to prevent any one person from dominating the group. As the cards are grouped based on the relationships, team members see that some ideas might be moved several times by different members of the group. Team members can begin to talk when only a few items remain. An item that is moved several times may need to be discussed and further subdivided onto other cards.

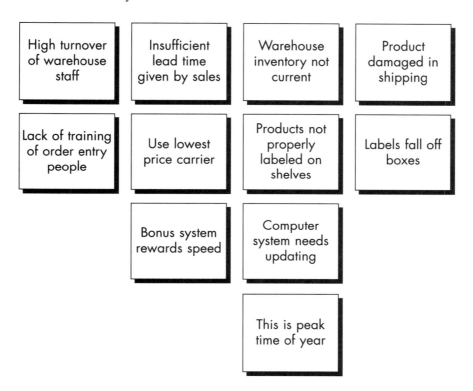

STEP 4. CREATE HEADINGS

The next step is to create headings for the groupings. These headings should capture the common element that represents why these items are grouped. Sometimes the brainstormed item can serve as the header.

TRAINING	POLICY	ORDER PROCESSING SYSTEM	PACKAGING

STEP 5. COMPLETE THE DIAGRAM

For the last step, add the original topic that focused the discussion in the first place. Do a final edit of the diagram by checking for repetitive items or adding other items if appropriate.

TOPIC: What are the reasons we are missing shipping dates?			
TRAINING	POLICY	ORDER PROCESSING SYSTEM	PACKAGING
High turnover of warehouse staff	Insufficient lead time given by sales	Warehouse inventory not current	Product damaged in shipping
Lack of training of order entry people	Use lowest price carrier	Products not properly labeled on shelves	Labels fall off boxes
	Bonus system rewards speed	Computer system needs updating	
		This is peak time of year	

W O R K S H E E T

WHAT'S IN IT FOR YOU?

• **Practice creating an Affinity Diagram on a real team issue**

PROBLEM SOLVING

10.8 Identifying the Problem — An Affinity Diagram Worksheet

STEP 1. STATE THE TOPIC

State the topic to be discussed. The main reason for the selection of the topic is that it contains many of the issues that concern the team members. Most people will have some relevant information to bring to the discussion.

Topic: _____

STEP 2. GENERATE AND LIST IDEAS

The second step is to generate ideas (see Worksheet 10.5 for questions to stimulate thinking) that help understand the issue and why it exists. These single ideas should be recorded on 3 x 5 cards or self-adhesive notes where they can be seen and reached by all team members.

STEP 3. GROUP THE IDEAS

At this point, team members should arrange the cards or self-adhesive notes into related groups *without discussion*. The silence is to prevent any one person from dominating the group. As the cards are grouped based on the relationships, team members see that some ideas might be moved several times by different members of the group. Team members can begin to talk when only a few items remain. An item that is moved several times may need to be discussed and further subdivided onto other cards.

STEP 4. CREATE HEADINGS

The next step is to create headings for the groupings. These headings should capture the common element that represents why these items are grouped. Sometimes the brainstormed item can serve as the header.

STEP 5. COMPLETE THE DIAGRAM

For the last step, add the original topic that focused the discussion in the first place. Do a final edit of the diagram by checking for repetitive items or adding other items if appropriate.

Topic: _____

Headings:

Groupings:

I D E A

PROBLEM SOLVING

10.9 Identifying the Problem — Writing a Problem Statement

After team members have answered the questions on the Worksheet for Identifying the Problem or completed an Affinity Diagram, they need to formulate a problem statement. It should be a short, clear, simple statement of the problem as most team members understand it. A problem statement is not a goal statement. Goal statements arise from the solutions chosen. The problem statement should not imply a solution.

A well-crafted problem statement will have these characteristics:

- The problem should be clearly stated so everyone can explore the aspects that are relevant to them.
- Moving to solutions at this time is premature and, therefore, the problem statement should be "unbiased" toward a solution.
- The problem statement should contain quantifiable information whenever possible. The process of gathering quantifiable data can substantiate or change assumptions and perceptions about the problem and may even point to a clearer picture of the solution.
- Before the completion of problem identification, the team will usually have to go outside the team or organization to obtain the necessary information. Don't rush it! Allow people to get the information they need to understand the issue.

I D E A

• **See the difference between a poorly written problem statement and a well-crafted one**

PROBLEM SOLVING

10.10 Identifying the Problem — Sample Problem Statements

Ineffective Problem Statement	More Effective Problem Statement
No one answers the phone around here.	A customer may typically hear the phone ring 5–7 times before someone will answer.
We don't have enough money to make our product.	Our monthly expenses exceed our monthly revenue by 3.2%.
We need more sales.	Our profit margins are running at .05% on $X\$$ of revenue.
We need to hire more salespeople.	So few salespeople are working the phones that 1 out of 4 customers hang up before talking to a salesperson.
We don't know who our customer is.	Our market segments are so unclear that we have not clearly defined our market strategies.
People are treated unfairly around here.	Seventeen out of 27 people who left this organization in the last 6 months listed dissatisfaction with their manager as the primary reason for leaving in the exit interview.

I D E A

• Understand why generating multiple ideas is critical to finding a good solution

PROBLEM SOLVING

10.11 The Second Step: Generating Alternatives

Points to remember after the problem has been identified and the team is trying to generate ideas:

- When groups fail to produce a solution or when the solution is inadequate, it usually results from the lack of alternative solutions generated by the team.
- There must be more than one alternative generated and considered — *alternatives* are plural.
- Encourage an atmosphere of "anything goes" or "throw away the givens" if true alternatives are to be found.
- The feasibility of the alternatives should not prohibit team members from voicing their ideas or alternatives.
- Define a specific process (see Ideas 10.12 and 10.13 on brainstorming) and time period to generate the possible alternatives, and stick to it! Don't be seduced into choosing a solution before all the possible alternatives have been generated and your team has examined the pros and cons of each alternative solution!

I D E A

• **Increase the number of alternatives to a problem through brainstorming**

PROBLEM SOLVING

10.12 Generating Alternatives — Brainstorming

Brainstorming is a time-proven technique that can be used by your team to encourage creative thinking and group synergy. It is a tactic for generating the greatest number of ideas in response to a given question. The ideas are recorded for further development and a feasibility check at a later date.

Brainstorming is used for the following reasons:

- Brainstorming encourages participation by all team members.
- It releases creativity through free association with others' ideas.
- It puts a premium on the generation of as many ideas as possible without the initial concern for quality.
- It takes the pressure off having to be "politically correct."
- It allows conflicting ideas to be voiced and made prominent without volatility.

Brainstorming might be ineffective in the following situations:

- The leader or team members evaluate individual contributions during the brainstorming period.
- Team members favor one idea over another during the brainstorming period.
- No one takes the time or effort to faithfully record individual team member ideas.

I D E A

• Conduct a brainstorming session to generate alternative solutions to a problem

PROBLEM SOLVING

10.13 Generating Alternatives — How to Brainstorm

These rules are essential for brainstorming to be productive and creative:

- Each team member tries to think of as many ideas (alternatives) as possible.
- Laughter is okay; criticism or evaluation, positive or negative, of the idea is not allowed.
- The stranger or wilder the idea, the better; it may provoke other ideas.
- Everyone participates.
- Discussion and analysis of the idea occur after the brainstorming session.
- Each team member tries to build on other ideas.

Team Leader Role

- Stimulate ideas.
- Ensure that team members follow the rules.
- Help phrase or frame the ideas.
- Ensure equal participation.

Steps in Brainstorming

- The leader sets the rules, clarifies the problem statement, and checks for understanding.
- A time limit is set (15 to 20 minutes, if appropriate).
- All ideas are recorded on chart paper, index cards, a chalkboard, etc.
- All ideas are encouraged; do not allow evaluative (negative or positive) comments.
- Allow any team member to say "pass."
- Clarify an idea, if needed, before it is recorded.
- Continue until everyone passes.
- Categorize ideas into themes or major alternatives to be evaluated and considered.

I D E A

• Discover why examining the pros and cons of alternatives is critical to discovering a workable solution to a problem

PROBLEM SOLVING

10.14 The Third Step: Examining Alternatives

After brainstorming a number of ideas, the team should use a preferred decision-making process* to determine the three to five major alternatives for further consideration. None of these major alternatives should be taken for granted. Look at each alternative and thoroughly examine the pros and cons. Each alternative will have its strengths and weaknesses; if it didn't, there would be no problem to solve.

The examination of the pros and cons of each alternative is important:

- Examination prevents steamrolling by one or two team members toward a solution which only they want.
- It helps anticipate future problems.
- The analysis may point the way to specific action steps that need to be taken.
- Examination may "expose" popular solutions that have unseen weaknesses.

The examination of pros and cons might be ineffective in emergency situations when there is not enough time to consider each alternative. This examination will also not work when a leader-dominated group chooses not to voice the "real" pros and cons.

*See Ideas 11.1–11.7 for information on decision-making strategies and processes.

I D E A

PROBLEM SOLVING

10.15 Examining Alternatives — The Force Field Analysis

A fascinating technique for analyzing the major alternative solutions to a problem is a Force Field Analysis. Through this approach, an alternative can be explored for its political correctness and its feasibility of working. Initially, each alternative is considered to be in a state of equilibrium or status quo — in other words, it is neither a good alternative nor a bad one, an easy one nor a hard one, an effective one nor an impotent one. The team's challenge is to examine the forces — both "driving" and "restraining" — that keep the alternative in equilibrium. The team can list the driving or restraining forces at the same time.

For example, say the problem the team is working on is

"Our monthly expenses exceed our monthly revenue by 3.2%."

One alternative solution is

"To sell 350 units of product X at a margin of 5% by X date."

This alternative solution would be discussed in the following terms:

• What are the driving forces working for this alternative to happen?
• What are the restraining forces working against this happening?

As the driving forces (pros) and restraining forces (cons) are listed, they are displayed as follows:

Alternative Solution: Sell 350 Units of Product X at 5%

←   →

Restraining Forces	Driving Forces
1. Just finished a big promotion on product X.	1. Certain regional locations have a bigger need because of weather conditions.
2. Competitors have lowered their prices in the past.	2. Customer survey says that our product is preferred 3 to 1 over others.
3. Warehouse has only 100 units in stock at this time.	
4. Just launched a new product, and sales is occupied with getting it off the ground.	
5. Just dropped the new catalog last month with old prices.	

The team would continue to list driving and restraining forces until no team member can think of any others.

Once the list is complete, team members should then go back and designate which restraining forces contribute most to the alternative not moving or changing.

If this alternative is chosen, then the group would want to take the restraining forces into consideration in the action plan.

I D E A

PROBLEM SOLVING

10.16 The Fifth Step: Choosing a Solution and Planning Action Steps

The team has identified the problem, generated alternatives, and examined and weighed the alternative solutions with their individual pros and cons. Now, the choice must be made.

Choice implies consideration of more than one alternative. Many teams fail to consider their alternatives and will go along with something proposed by one member because of fear or respect or because they don't want to hurt someone's feelings. In either case, the solution may be less than effective.

Choosing the solution is the decisive step. Choosing the best alternative necessitates comparing basic assumptions, goals, and consequences. It requires asking the final questions, why and what if, as a final check.

Deciding is, of course, done through consensus.* While it may not always be possible to reach consensus, commitment from all group members is essential.

Once the solution can be supported by team members, action steps need to be generated and an action plan put into place.

Resources you might find helpful include:

- Mind mapping is a nonlinear method for generating ideas (action steps) that can then be organized into a chronological order. Tony Buzan's book *The Mind Map Book* is very helpful for teaching mind mapping.
- Gantt Project Planning charts and their modern counterparts can be used to map out a detailed plan to achieve targeted outcomes.
  Gantt Charts measure progress against a schedule, the load required on departments, people, machines, etc., and availability of resources and are plotted in relationship to time.
- PERT (Performance Evaluation and Review Technique) planning and CPM (Critical Path Methods) are used for complex projects that require a coordinated plan involving activities and scheduling and deploying resources.

*See Ideas 11.6 and 11.7 on reaching consensus.

IDEA

WHAT'S IN IT FOR YOU?

- **Discover proven and creative problem-solving techniques from a variety of texts and journals**

PROBLEM SOLVING

10.17 Bibliography

Buzan, T. *Use Both Sides of Your Brain.* New York: E.P. Dutton, Inc., 1983.

Buzan, T. *The Mind Map Book.* New York: E.P. Dutton, Inc., 1994.

Chang, R., and P.K. Kelly. *Step-by-Step Problem-Solving.* Irvine, CA: Richard Chang Associates, Inc., 1993.

Cowan, D.A. "Developing a Process Model of Problem Recognition," *Academy of Management Review* (October 1986): 763–776.

Golin, M. "How to Brainstorm by Yourself ... and Triple the Results," *Young Executive* (Spring 1992): 75.

Higgins, J.M. *101 Creative Problem-Solving Techniques: The Handbook of New Ideas for Business.* Winter Park, FL: New Management Publishing Company, Inc., 1994.

Kepner, C., and B. Tregoe. *The New Rational Manager.* New York: McGraw-Hill, 1989.

Lewin, D. *Field Theory and Social Science: Selected Theoretical Papers.* New York: Harper and Row, 1951.

Stein, M.I. *Stimulating Creativity: Group Procedure.* New York: Academic Press, 1975.

Van Gundy, A.B. *Creative Problem Solving: A Guide for Trainers and Management.* New York: Quorum Books, 1987.

Wycoff, J. *Mind Mapping.* New York: Berkeley Publishing Group, 1991.

CHAPTER ELEVEN

DECISION-MAKING STRATEGIES

WHAT'S IN IT FOR YOU?

- **Learn why it's important to have an accepted decision-making process**
- **Determine which of the five types of decision making is best suited for various team issues**
- **Follow six guiding principles for reaching consensus when you need support from all team members on a particular decision**

Even when your team doesn't make a decision, it's unwittingly made a decision. Bringing a group of diverse people to the same understanding and conclusions on issues can be a frustrating and time-consuming ordeal. Not all decisions warrant such attention; others demand it. This chapter will help your team determine if the leader decides, majority rule, minority rule, "plop," or consensus is the best way to make a decision.

I D E A

DECISION-MAKING STRATEGIES

11.1 Decisions, Decisions!

Decision-making strategies are options that help the team decide what, how, how much, and when work gets done by the team. Many times, teams will not straightforwardly make a decision. Then, the old adage, "no decision is a decision," applies. The problem is that no one is clear, and heated misunderstandings result.

There are five standard ways of purposefully deciding on an issue:

- Consensus; majority rules; minority rules; leader decides; decision by plop

The size and type of the team will influence the type of decision making that is feasible. The issue to be decided and its relative importance to the team's outcomes will determine the type of decision making that is most appropriate.

As team leader, you need to guide your group to choose an accepted decision-making strategy for the following reasons:

- Lack of clear decision making over time would drastically reduce the work group's effectiveness.
- Without an accepted decision-making strategy, team members may tend to advocate a strategy that serves their ends only.
- Without a clear decision-making strategy, issues could be discussed over and over again with no closure.

As you consider the types of decisions your team will face in the future, consider how the team has made decisions in the past:

- Has there been a tendency to use one decision-making strategy over another?
- Has the type of decision making been appropriate?
- Is the team aware of how it's making decisions and the impact one strategy may have over another?

I D E A

• **Consider which decisions your team should be making by majority vote**

DECISION-MAKING STRATEGIES

11.2 The Majority Rules

With the majority rules decision-making process, team members vote *yes* or *no*, and after a count, the decision is made. Depending upon team size, abstentions may be allowed. Most people, living in a democracy, understand the "weight of numbers process."

Use majority rules in these situations:

- Time is of concern. Majority rules is fast.
- A decision must be made. With majority rules, a decision can be reached, assuming there are no tie votes.
- A majority of the team needs to be committed to the decision, at least tacitly.
- A simple, understood decision-making process is required. Most people understand majority rules.

A majority rules strategy will be ineffective in the following situations:

- Commitment by all members is needed to implement the decision.
- No decision is reached because of a tie.
- The minority has most of the economic and political power.
- The majority-rules strategy is used to oppress the minority.

I D E A

• Consider on which issues your team should let the minority rule

DECISION-MAKING STRATEGIES

11.3 The Minority Rules

With this decision-making strategy, a small group within the group decides the issue. The biggest advantage to minority rules is that a concerned minority can have its needs met in the face of an apathetic majority. Of course, that is also the biggest liability of a minority rules strategy: because the majority is apathetic, uninformed, or divided, the minority "carries the day." The minority could lobby "behind the scenes," and when a vote is taken, some team members abstain in order for the minority to win.

Use a minority rules strategy in these situations:

- Time is of the essence. This strategy is fast.
- A decision must be reached. Voting provides a clear winner.
- The minority members are better informed, capable, and qualified to make the decision.
- The majority lacks commitment and wants to abdicate or not indicate a preference.
- Team members want to use abstention as a trade-off.

A minority rules strategy will be ineffective when commitment by all team members is needed to implement the decision. It can also backfire when apathetic or uninformed members realize — after the decision is reached — that the implications of the decision are not in the team's best interests.

I D E A

- **Consider when you, as team leader, should be the decision maker**
- **Understand the advantages and pitfalls of making decisions for your team**

DECISION-MAKING STRATEGIES

11.4 The Leader Decides

This decision-making strategy involves the hierarchical, appointed, or designated leader deciding what the team should do. In most cases, the leader takes into consideration the thoughts of various team members and, because of position power, expertise power, or ownership, makes the decision. If "Solomon is at the helm," the decision may be wise; if not ...

Having the leader decide is effective in the following situations:

- The fastest strategy is needed — assuming you're a decisive leader.
- A decision must be reached.
- The leader bears the brunt of the decision.
- Team members want to abstain without indicating a preference.
- Leader control is high and can lower the team's risks.
- The leader can protect the team's interests.

Having the leader decide will be ineffective in these situations:

- Commitment by all team members is needed to implement the decision.
- The development of team member involvement is important for future decisions.
- The leader's decision lacks information or perspective, or it serves limited self-interest.
- The leader does not have the technical expertise to address the issue.
- The strategy is used to cut off debate or comprehensive examination of alternatives.
- Deference to authority occurs, and team members withdraw from the examination of the issue.

I D E A

- **Recognize when a nondecision is a good decision**
- **Consider how not making decisions will thwart team progress**

DECISION-MAKING STRATEGIES

11.5 Decision by Plop

In this strategy, no one chooses to make the decision, or people agree, tacitly, not to decide. So, the question is just "plopped" and no decision becomes the decision. Over time, the repeated use of this approach is to invite a "rudderless" condition in which the team has no consistent direction. Issues languish in Never-Never-Land and die of benign neglect.

Use a Decision by Plop strategy in the following situations:

- There's no time to make a decision. This strategy is fast (so to speak).
- It's not worth the possible conflict between team members.
- No one wants to take responsibility for the decision.
- Time for further analysis is needed.
- The issue may be insignificant enough not to warrant deliberation.
- The issue may be politically volatile enough to warrant avoidance by all team members.

A Decision by Plop strategy will be ineffective in these situations:

- A clear, emphatic decision is needed for the team to do its work.
- Team member conflict is so feared that the issue becomes the casualty.
- Decision by Plop is symptomatic of other unaccepted decisions made in the past.
- A Plop decision is the result of lack of team member commitment.

I D E A

• **Understand the nature of decision making by consensus**
• **Determine which issues are worth the effort of building consensus**

DECISION-MAKING STRATEGIES

11.6 Consensus

Consensus is a process through which the issue is decided by agreement of all members. It implies that all team members are willing to pledge their commitment and support. Not everyone must have initially favored the decision, but at the point of decision, everyone must be willing to make a commitment to support it.

Consensus is agreement based on a discussion with true appreciation of the other points of view concerning the issue(s). Consensus is not compromise, abdication, unanimity, or deference. If a team member can't commit, discussion continues until commitment is given.

Use a consensus strategy in the following situations:

- The issue requires team member commitment.
- It's important that all team members understand the issue.
- All team member viewpoints can be drawn out.
- The collective wisdom of all members can be tapped to solve the issue.
- All team members assume responsibility for the success of the solution.

A consensus strategy will be ineffective in these situations:

- There is not enough time available for discussion and understanding of the issues.
- No decision is reached because of team members' failure to commit.
- A leader overrules the decision.
- Team members fail to keep their commitments.

IDEA

• **Learn how to guide your team to consensus decisions**

DECISION-MAKING STRATEGIES

11.7 Six Guiding Principles for Reaching Consensus

1. Team members should try not to argue for their position in order to "win." The best decision is one that captures the collective wisdom of the team.

2. Conflict during discussion should be seen as aiding the exploration of the issue rather than delaying the upcoming "call" for consensus.

3. The process of consensus should be facilitated by periodic "checks" with each team member to determine if people are ready for a decision. At the point of decision making, each team member should be willing to say, "I can support the decision."

4. Each team member must take responsibility for listening to all points of view and for voicing his or her own views. The "proof" of listening is in being able to paraphrase all points of view.

5. Each team member should help monitor the balance between engaging in meaningful conflict, which leads to full exploration of the issues, and avoiding conflict, which is based on the fear of conflict in general.

6. Consensus, in its best form, stems not only from viable, believable solutions, but also from team members whose emotions are at rest and in tune with the solutions chosen.

CHAPTER TWELVE

CONFLICT RESOLUTION STRATEGIES

WHAT'S IN IT FOR YOU?

- Understand why having a process for dealing with conflict, rather than just good intentions, leads to better resolution
- Increase your understanding of why conflict happens
- Realize the choices for handling conflict
- Provide team members with a conflict resolution worksheet to help alleviate the emotional element of conflict
- Prevent "groupthink"
- Refer to additional resources to enhance conflict management skill

C ontrary to what you might think, conflict can be a very good thing. The difference between most groups and a HIT is that a HIT appreciates conflict and follows a systematic process for resolving it. This chapter will help you personally and as a team leader to resolve conflict through accepting, creating, retreating, contesting, or modifying depending on the situation.

I D E A

• Value conflict as a necessary agent for developing a team

CONFLICT RESOLUTION STRATEGIES

12.1 Conflict Happens

While conflict may not be something you want to go looking for, team members should consider conflict as positive. Teams that have little or no conflict throughout the team's life may lack passion for and commitment to their work. Conflict usually results from differing values, viewpoints, and knowledge bases among the team members. Those differences should be treasured as the basis for better creative solutions.

Conflict resolution strategies are steps or actions that help team members work through conflict arising from differing views about what the team's work is and how the team should accomplish the work. Helpful conflict resolution strategies should lead to more collaborative work solutions and more positive team member relationships.

Having a process or strategy to follow in times of conflict is helpful for the following reasons:

- Conflict resolution strategies help team members put their egos aside in favor of the team purpose and outcomes.
- These strategies help individual team members to merge ideas.
- They help team members learn more about themselves.
- They lead to greater goal and task clarity for the team members.
- They help team members be more comfortable with necessary differences in viewpoints.

Conflict resolution strategies may be ineffective under the following conditions:

- Control over rewards and punishments is unevenly distributed among team members.
- An individual team member's self-esteem is so low that no forgiveness is possible between individuals.
- The organized culture allows for retribution outside the context of the team functions.

Does your team need or have conflict resolution strategies? Consider these questions:

- How does your team handle conflict now? Is it encouraged, leveraged, accepted, and expected; or is it avoided, hushed, buried, and demeaned?
- Does the team tend to always handle conflict in the same way, or does it have a variety of methods for dealing with the many kinds of conflict that may arise?
- Is the team aware of the source and types of conflict likely to surface?

In order for conflict to be of value, the team must first consider it of value, then be clear on the strategies for dealing with it appropriately.

I D E A

WHAT'S IN IT FOR YOU?

• **Be able to determine the cause or source of conflict**

CONFLICT RESOLUTION STRATEGIES

12.2 Five Basic Reasons for Conflict

Differences in Beliefs and Values

- Team members have different moral, ideological, or philosophical beliefs.

Role Pressures

- Team members develop attitudes about what they should or should not do in their roles.
- Team members must represent and remain loyal to a constituency outside the team.

Perceptual Differences

- People who have had different experiences with similar situations filter their current perceptions of those experiences.
- Team members sometimes mistake perceptual differences for stubbornness, hidden agendas, or stupidity, which then brings the conflict to a personal level.
- People do not take differing (or conflicting) personality or disposition types into account, assuming that other team members see things the same way they do.

Different Goals

- Resources in the form of money, personnel, and time are limited, and team members may compete for them to serve their own ends.
- Team members may protect their own unit's turf and interpret the organization's goals to serve their own goals.

Status

- Team members may use the team to gain individual recognition.
- Team members may use team activities to further career opportunities.

I D E A

WHAT'S IN IT FOR YOU?

- **Increase the ways you currently deal with conflict**
- **Realize that there are choices of how conflict can be resolved**

CONFLICT RESOLUTION STRATEGIES

12.3 Five Strategies for Resolving Conflict

When it comes to conflict, an individual's behavior can fall into two basic categories:

1. High or low amounts of self-oriented needs (assertiveness)
2. High or low amounts of other-oriented needs (cooperation).

These behaviors are not either/or but can occur at the same time, as indicated in the matrix: *

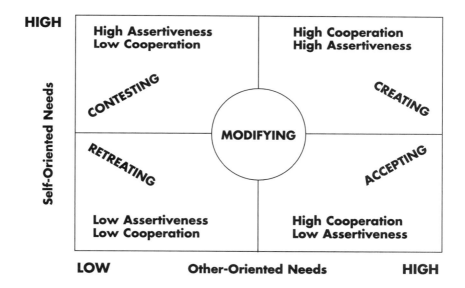

The frequent or infrequent occurrence of these two types of behaviors results in five ways of resolving conflict:

- Accepting; Creating; Contesting; Retreating; Modifying

Each of these ways of resolving conflict can be useful, depending upon the situation and the perceived importance of the issues to the individuals.

---

*This model has been adapted from "Conflict and Conflict Management" by Kenneth Thomas in *The Handbook of Industrial and Organizational Psychology*, Marvin Dunnette, ed. (Chicago: Rand McNally, 1976).

I D E A

- **Determine when accepting is the most appropriate strategy for dealing with a conflict**

CONFLICT RESOLUTION STRATEGIES

12.4 Accepting

With the Accepting strategy of conflict resolution, individuals tend to set aside their own concerns to meet the needs of others. Accepting is the result of low amounts of assertive behaviors and high amounts of cooperative behaviors. This "you win, I lose" approach contains elements of giving and self-sacrifice.

Why use this strategy?

- You want to be seen as fair and able to give.
- The "stakes" are low or unimportant to you.
- You have no control, and the decision is already made.
- You want to build I.O.U.'s for another issue.
- Team cohesiveness and togetherness are more important.
- You want other team members to try other ideas that might work.
- You are unsure of your own solutions or ideas about the issue.

What are the characteristics of the Accepting strategy?

- One party always ends up being the "loser."
- The "winner" may view the loser with disdain or mistrust.
- Resolution may imply "I'll collect mine at a later time."
- The strategy may become inflexible if it's used exclusively over time.

When can the Accepting strategy be ineffective?

- Your input or solutions are not getting the consideration that you want or the team needs.
- Some group members have taken advantage of your goodwill in the past.
- You think the issue is too important to experiment with.
- You resent the individual(s) and think the conflict is unresolved, and you hope the conflict will just go away.

I D E A

- **Determine when creating is the most appropriate strategy for dealing with a conflict**

CONFLICT RESOLUTION STRATEGIES

12.5 Creating

The Creating strategy for resolving conflict finds a solution in which the needs of both parties have been met and satisfied. Creating is a result of high amounts of assertive behaviors and high amounts of cooperative behaviors. This means that both parties must know enough about each other's needs and concerns to mutually create solutions that are unanticipated at the onset of the conflict.

Why use this strategy?
- Both parties consider the issue too important to compromise.
- Ideas, which by themselves would be inadequate, can be synthesized.
- You can involve others in blending several ideas.
- It's possible to produce something innovative or creative.
- You can improve your ideas or test the limits of your ideas.
- You can gain the commitment of others to implement solutions.

What are the characteristics of the Creating strategy?
- Both parties must affirm the basis of each other's objectives.
- The objectives of each party are fully achieved.
- The needs of each party are met without hardship to either one.
- Energy is focused on the issue, not on each other.
- A certain amount of disclosure and support is necessary.
- The solution is seen as a "win-win" by the team members.
- Creating demands time to explore ideas and relationships.

When can the Creating strategy be ineffective?
- There is little time for discussion.
- Interpersonal trust and disclosure are not possible.
- Team members represent constituencies who will not accept the created solution.
- One person's perception of his or her power in the situation allows that person to retract the promise of cooperation
- The importance of the issue does not warrant the amount of time it will take to resolve.

IDEA

- **Determine when retreating is the most appropriate strategy for dealing with a conflict**

CONFLICT RESOLUTION STRATEGIES

12.6 Retreating

In the Retreating strategy, the individual chooses not to deal with the conflict. Retreating is apparent when a team member displays low amounts of cooperative behaviors and low amounts of assertive behaviors. The individual may opt to withdraw, put off the issue for another day, or tactfully reframe the issue to make it a nonissue.

Why use this strategy?
- There are no apparent possible solutions.
- Time or other circumstances may resolve the conflict.
- The issue is of minor importance.
- The issue is a "sidebar" to a larger core issue.
- More facts or data need to be collected.
- A cooling-off period is needed for more rational heads to prevail.
- The benefits of a resolution are outweighed by the potential damage of confrontation.

What are the characteristics of the Retreating strategy?
- Either or both parties refuse to deal with the issue or the conflict at the time.
- The interpersonal conflict is driven below the surface of future interactions between the conflicting team members.
- Many "I should have said" conversations take place with uninvolved parties.

When can the Retreating strategy be ineffective?
- A more legitimate strategy can be used at that time.
- A decision will be made by default.
- An inappropriate amount of energy is given to cautious, inauthentic, time-consuming behaviors.
- The habitual use of the strategy leads to a lack of commitment to and passion for the team's outcomes.

IDEA

- Determine when a contesting strategy is the most appropriate for dealing with a conflict

CONFLICT RESOLUTION STRATEGIES

12.7 Contesting

With the Contesting strategy for resolving conflict, an individual is concerned with winning at the expense of another's concerns or needs. Contesting is a result of frequent use of high assertiveness and low cooperative behaviors. This strategy pits power against power so that the capacity to use sanctions, withdraw support, or use one's position produces the solution to the conflict. A team member may want to "stick up for his or her ideas" or just show the ability to win.

Why use this strategy?
- Fast, definite action is essential because the stakes are high or there is an emergency situation.
- It's mandatory to win the current conflict, regardless of long-term consequences.
- It's necessary to guard against those who would exploit noncontesting behavior.
- The spirit of competition unites the team to strive harder.

What are the characteristics of the Contesting strategy?
- The strategy may be seen by team members as a struggle for dominance.
- Contesting may have an adverse effect on trust between team members.
- Consequences may be disregarded in the "heat of battle."
- This approach contains an element of "If we can't play with my ball, then we won't play at all."
- The conflict may cause a greater conflict in the future.

When can the Contesting strategy be ineffective?
- You want to develop others' ideas and initiatives.
- You are unsure of your ideas.
- You don't have the power necessary to win.
- You need the commitment of others to implement the solutions.
- The emotional tone created in team meetings, as a result of contesting, restrains the free exchange of ideas in the future.

I D E A

• Determine when the modifying strategy is the most appropriate for dealing with a conflict

CONFLICT RESOLUTION STRATEGIES

12.8 Modifying

The Modifying strategy for conflict resolution leads to a give-and-take approach in which both parties get enough of what they want to be satisfied, but not necessarily all. Modifying is achieved when an individual uses moderate amounts of both assertive and cooperative behaviors. The solution results in concessions from both sides, and a compromise is accepted.

Why use this strategy?

- It appears to be the most "expedient" possibility.
- All other strategies have failed.
- Power is evenly distributed between the two conflicting parties, and their goals are mutually exclusive.
- The issues are moderately important, and contesting is too disturbing to the team's future work.

What are the characteristics of the Modifying strategy?

- Each side gets some of what it wants; neither side gets all that it wants.
- There must be enough trust to believe that each party will live up to its side of the bargain.
- Modifying requires an understanding of the constraints under which each party operates.
- The parties must enter the compromise realizing that the solution will give them less than what they want.

When can the Modifying strategy be ineffective?

- You will be viewed by team members as self-centered and nongiving.
- The issues are too important to make trade-offs, which then modify your solution to the point that it is no longer viable.

I D E A

CONFLICT RESOLUTION STRATEGIES

12.9 The First Rule in Conflict Resolution

Managing conflict is not just the responsibility of the team leader. All team members should be responsible. But, most team members do not know what to do in the following circumstances:

1. They observe an interpersonal blowup between two people on the team.

2. They sense an interpersonal conflict between two people, but it has not surfaced.

Ask your team members to follow these simple, but not necessarily easy, steps to begin conflict resolution and prevent the team from becoming a spectator in a private clash.

If the conflict is public, the first rule in conflict resolution is to slow it down.

- Ask the conflicting parties to please be quiet.
- Ask one party to state his or her point of view. Tell the listening party that he or she cannot rebut or explain until he or she has paraphrased what has been said.
- Once a paraphrase has been done and checked for accuracy, the second party may then describe or explain his or her point of view.

If the conflict is sensed but has not surfaced, the first rule in conflict resolution is to confirm or deny the conflict exists.

- Ask the parties involved if the team norm of resolving conflicts is being met or if there are issues that should be voiced.
- Help the parties determine if the conflict is best resolved together with the team's input or dealt with privately as an interpersonal issue.
- Remind the parties of their choices for conflict resolution strategies.
- Help them determine which of the strategies best represents this particular situation.
- If the parties can't agree on how the conflict should be managed and it could affect a team issue, the team may decide to use a problem-solving strategy for resolving the situation.

W O R K S H E E T

CONFLICT RESOLUTION STRATEGIES

12.10 Conflict Resolution Worksheet

Getting to the resolution of conflict involves the true understanding of four elements of the conflict:

1. The issue
2. Your position
3. The other party's position
4. The context of the issue.

Use the following set of questions to review these key elements in order to plan and resolve a conflict you or your team may have.

1. The Issue

• Define the issue. What is the real situation? What is the "ideal"?

2. Your Position

• Describe the conflict from your point of view. List your needs and wants, your proposed solution, and why you think your solution will work.

• How much power do you have in this conflict?

1   2   3   4   5   6   7   8   9   10

• How much do you trust this person or each party?

1   2   3   4   5   6   7   8   9   10

- How important is the resolution of this issue to you?

1   2   3   4   5   6   7   8   9   10

- How much time is there to discuss the issues around this conflict?

1   2   3   4   5   6   7   8   9   10

- List the actual behaviors of the other party that contribute to the conflict.

3. The Other Party's Position

- Explain what you think the other person wants and needs, what you think his or her proposed solution is, and why you think it will and won't work.

- How much power does the other person have in this conflict?

1   2   3   4   5   6   7   8   9   10

- How much does the other person trust you?

1   2   3   4   5   6   7   8   9   10

- How important is the resolution of this issue to the other person?

1   2   3   4   5   6   7   8   9   10

- How much time does the other person think is available to discuss the issue?

1   2   3   4   5   6   7   8   9   10

• List the behaviors you think the other person would say you exhibit that contribute to the conflict.

4. The Context of the Issue

• List the things, people, policies, procedures, etc., that may be contributing to the conflict.

• What is the basis of the problem? (Check one.)
  ❑ Differences in beliefs and values   ❑ Different goals
  ❑ Role pressures   ❑ Status
  ❑ Perceptual differences

Based on the analysis of the above elements, check which five of the conflict resolution strategies is the most feasible:

	Not Feasible	Somewhat Feasible	Most Feasible
Accepting	❑	❑	❑
Creating	❑	❑	❑
Contesting	❑	❑	❑
Retreating	❑	❑	❑
Modifying	❑	❑	❑

Which conflict resolution strategy do you choose?

Using this strategy, what actions do you plan?

I D E A

CONFLICT RESOLUTION STRATEGIES

12.11 Preventing Groupthink

Groupthink is in evidence when the team is more focused on avoiding conflict than it is on finding creative, better, or alternative ideas and solutions.

Groupthink happens when team members strive so hard for agreement that they override individual members who try to seek realistic alternatives. A team focused and driven to reach a decision may ignore various points of view, ideas, or key data that could alter the tact the team is bent on pursuing. Sometimes, consensus is so important that it can override the critical thinking of various members of the team.

Why is groupthink so important to avoid?

- Team discussions are limited to one or two alternatives without a full understanding of all the possibilities that could be considered.
- The team chooses not to reexamine the course of action initially preferred by most members, which may contain hidden risks and drawbacks.
- Little attempt is made to obtain information or opinions from experts outside the group who may shed light upon alternative courses of action.
- There may be a selective bias to factual data and information. Positive interest may be shown for information and ideas that support the prevailing position; other ideas are ignored.

What are the conditions that spawn groupthink?

- Pressure from vested interests outside the group pushing for decisions to be made, even if the group has little time or data to make a quality decision.
- The team's norms emphasize speed and confidence.
- The internal process of the group prevents key individuals on the team, who have opinions that are contrary to the team's decision, to speak up.
- The team is a leader-dominated group, and it will not engage in an open dialogue to reach decisions.

I D E A

WHAT'S IN IT FOR YOU?

• **Take steps to prevent groupthink.**

CONFLICT RESOLUTION STRATEGIES

12.12 Eight Strategies for Preventing Groupthink

1. Support frank discussions by asking team members to discuss alternatives with associates back in their units and share reactions with the team.
2. After a tentative decision has been reached concerning the chosen alternative, have a special meeting to allow each member to share, as loudly and clearly as possible, any lingering doubts.
3. Have the team review the logic that led to the decision.
4. Invite one or more outside experts or qualified people to every meeting.
5. Have one or more team members "take the side" of the rival group or unit that the issue will affect in order to simulate the possible effects or reactions.
6. Assign a process observer who will look for signs of groupthink.
7. Risk duplication of effort by having multiple groups working on similar issues (when the stakes are high enough).
8. Rotate leadership so that the leader abstains from presenting a personal position.

I D E A

WHAT'S IN IT FOR YOU?

- Take six steps that will remove the "silo barriers" from a cross-functional team

CONFLICT RESOLUTION STRATEGIES

12.13 Removing Silo Barriers

When forming cross-functional teams, the biggest potential source of conflict occurs when individual team members represent their functional area rather than the team's purpose or goals. If unity is not established, "silo barriers" will form, and rather than focusing on a common goal, individual team members will be "out for themselves." Work must be done in the chartering meetings* to ensure that a common project goal is formed that requires team member interdependence. In other words, the only way the goal will be achieved is through mutual cooperation.

1. In the chartering process, ensure that a common project goal is formed that requires the functional expertise of each team member to accomplish. Each member must see that there is organizational merit to the common good.

2. Each functional representative must let go of personal "functional bias" in order to commit to a common team goal. Encourage team members to discuss their functional concerns off-line with other department or functional members.

3. Ask functional representatives to return to the team to share/communicate the fears and negative implications that were voiced by the other members of the functional areas.

4. Team discussions should center around the possible implications for a negative impact on certain functions. Team member awareness must also be developed to show that dominance by one function could endanger team success.

5. Constructive conflict must result that helps all team members understand the merits and drawbacks of each functional point of view, while never forgetting the common team good.

6. Time must be allotted to build consensus toward the common goal while finding positive solutions to possible problems that have been created for functional units as a result of the project output or process.

*See Ideas 8.1–8.28 to review the process of creating a charter for your team.

IDEA

CONFLICT RESOLUTION STRATEGIES

12.14 Bibliography

Bramson, R. *Coping with Difficult People.* New York: Ballantine Books, 1981.

Costantino, C.A., and C.S. Merchant. *Designing Conflict Management Systems.* San Francisco: Jossey-Bass, Inc., 1997.

Crum, T.F. *The Magic of Conflict: Turning a Life of Work into a Work of Art.* New York: Simon and Schuster, 1987.

De Bono, E. *Conflicts: A Better Way to Resolve Them.* New York: Penguin Books, 1985.

How to Manage Conflict: A Quick and Handy Guide for Any Manager or Business Owner. Hawthorne, NJ: Career Press, 1993.

Kabanoff, B. "Potential Influence Structures as Sources of Interpersonal Conflict in Groups and Organizations," *Organizational Behavior and Human Decision Processes* 36 (1985): 113–141.

Kilmann, R.H., and K.W. Thomas. "Interpersonal Conflict-Handling Behavior as a Reflection of Jungian Personality Dimensions," *Psychological Reports* 37 (1975): 971–980.

Rothman, J. *Resolving Identity-Based Conflict in Nations, Organizations, and Communities.* San Francisco: Jossey-Bass, Inc., 1997.

Slaikeu, K.A. *When Push Comes to Shove: A Practical Guide to Mediating Disputes.* San Francisco: Jossey-Bass, Inc., 1994.

Thomas, Kenneth. "Conflict and Conflict Management," in *The Handbook of Industrial and Organizational Psychology,* Marvin Dunnette, ed. Chicago: Rand McNally, 1976.

Thomas, K.W., and W.H. Schmidt. "A Survey of Managerial Interests with Respect to Conflict," *Academy of Management Journal* 19 (1976): 315–318.

Ury, W.L.; J.M. Brett; and S.B. Goldberg. *Getting Disputes Resolved: Designing Systems to Cut the Cost of Conflict.* San Francisco: Jossey-Bass, Inc., 1993.

CHAPTER THIRTEEN

COMMUNICATION

WHAT'S IN IT FOR YOU?

- **Appreciate the complexity and dynamics of inter-team communication**
- **Become more aware of what your nonverbals are saying**
- **Practice four basic listening skills**
- **Try fun and unique techniques for improving communication during team meetings**
- **Determine the level of confidentiality needed to win and sustain trust**

Ask almost anybody about what needs improving in most organizations and the number one response will be, "communication." We have trouble communicating one-to-one with people we love, proven by the proliferation of bestselling books on the topic. Imagine the complexity communication takes on in a team with diverse ideas, backgrounds, genders, learning styles, and personality types. The least you can do as a team leader is monitor and work hard on your own communication skills. In this chapter you will be reminded that what you say is important, but it's the way you say it that matters most. You will also increase your proficiency in the most important communication skill of a team leader: listening by learning to paraphrase, ask questions, reflect feelings, and summarize.

IDEA

• **Acknowledge that communication skills must be taught, practiced, and refined**

COMMUNICATION

13.1 Did You Say Something?

Communicating is something we have all done since birth — indeed, perhaps even before. Yet, poor communication is credited for the majority of conflicts, problems, and discontent that come between people. The truth is, most of us have not had the training or feedback necessary to communicate effectively.

In a team setting, communication becomes even more problematic and complex. It seems simple enough: communication in a team setting is the clear, meaningful exchange of information about the team purpose, task purpose, task, and actions. However, whether we communicate face-to-face, on paper, or through electronic means, we can be effective or downright ineffective in the way we communicate. Because of their differing values, needs, and experiences, team members vary in how, when, and why they communicate with others the way they do.

It's important to improve your own and your team's communication skills for the following reasons:

- Effective communication can reduce tension.
- It can increase individual and team interaction.
- It can improve individual and team output.
- It can increase efficiency.
- It can increase self-understanding.
- Training can clarify team member obligations for communication.

There are five specific skills you need to refine in order to communicate well:

1. Showing appropriate attending behavior (nonverbal communication)
2. Paraphrasing
3. Reflecting feelings
4. Asking open-ended and closed questions
5. Summarizing.

It is also important to recognize the filters or obstacles that might exist (sometimes legitimately) that hamper effective communication — even when effective skills are used. Consider the following examples of filters/obstacles:

- Incongruous verbals and nonverbals
- Basic disagreement in values
- Lack of technical understanding
- Little or no preparation for meetings
- Interference from noise or outside disturbances
- Language or cultural barriers
- Personality or disposition-based behavior, such as introversion or extroversion.

I D E A

COMMUNICATION

13.2 Attending Behaviors

When communicating, it is critical to use the appropriate *attending behaviors*. When used effectively, these nonverbal behaviors will

- project interest, alertness, friendliness, relaxation, recognition, and non-judgment.
- help someone else understand your intentions.
- convey to others that you are listening or paying attention to them.

Observing someone else's attending behaviors is important because these behaviors

- give you a sense of what the other person is thinking or feeling about what you are saying.
- can help you sense if a person is withdrawing, is distressed, or needs help.

Interpreting another person's attending behaviors can backfire if

- the same nonverbal behavior means something different in a different culture.
- the nonverbal behavior is assumed to mean something, but it is not checked out with the individual.

I D E A

WHAT'S IN IT FOR YOU?

- **Identify four sources of nonverbal communication and what they can mean**

COMMUNICATION

13.3 Attending Behaviors — What You Don't Say Speaks Louder Than Your Words

There are four sources of attending behaviors that can convey "Go ahead," "Proceed with caution," or "Stop":

- Facial expressions — the frequency and duration of smiles, frowns, etc.
- Eye contact — the frequency and duration of direct eye contact
- Body positions — the positioning of legs, arms, shoulders, head, and hands
- Voice tone — the volume and inflection of a person's voice and the amount and speed of speech

"GO AHEAD" ATTENDING BEHAVIORS

Source	Nonverbal Expression
Face	smiles, friendly nodding
Eyes	direct contact, steady gaze
Arms	relaxed and open
Hands	at rest, relaxed and open
Legs	uncrossed or crossed toward you
Body angle	upright or directed toward you
Voice tone	responding with moderate volume and cadence

"PROCEED WITH CAUTION" ATTENDING BEHAVIORS

Source	Nonverbal Expression
Face	tense, skeptical, guarded, frustrated
Eyes	looking away, directing gaze to the speaker's eyebrows
Arms	crossed, tense
Hands	clasped, fidgeting with objects or parts of body
Legs	crossed away from you
Body angle	leaning away from you
Voice tone	low, soft, halting

"STOP" ATTENDING BEHAVIORS

Source	Nonverbal Expression
Face	scowling, yawning, excessive silence
Eyes	staring, glaring, excessive avoidance
Arms	crossed, tense, fidgeting
Hands	palms facing you, pointed fingers
Legs	crossed away from you
Body angle	turns back, walks away, or invades space
Voice tone	loud, rapid, clenched teeth

I D E A

- **Practice four of the most basic of communication skills**

COMMUNICATION

13.4 The Four Basic Communication Skills

There are four basic skills in the process of communicating that are demonstrable and should be used frequently to be seen as a good communicator and active listener.

1. **Paraphrasing.** Paraphrasing is the skill of stating in the individual's own words, as much as possible, exactly what was said by the speaker. The closer you come to the actual words and phrases used by the speaker, the more accurate the paraphrase. This will demonstrate that you are indeed listening. However, another point in paraphrasing is to demonstrate that you understand the underlying meaning of the words you heard. Demonstrating that you understand may require restating what you heard in your own words. The danger in restating is imbuing the statement with your personal twist or point of view. It is important to listen, paraphrase, and restate without prejudging what you hear.

2. **Reflecting feelings.** This is the skill of capturing the speaker's feeling or sentiment and restating it in nonjudgmental terms back to the speaker.

3. **Questioning.** The ability to ask open-ended questions is a skill that opens up the conversation. Response is usually prompted by "Why," "How," "Where," "Describe," or "Tell me more. ..." Closed questions can be used in very specific circumstances to bring closure to or direct a conversation, but in general they will not be regarded as a supportive behavior.

4. **Summarizing.** Summarizing is the skill of stating in capsule form what has been said over longer periods of time (20 minutes to an hour). Exact words are not as important in a summary as the order and sequence of what has been said. Note-taking not only can help in summarizing, but also, if other attending behaviors are not sacrificed, can demonstrate that you have been listening.

I D E A

WHAT'S IN IT FOR YOU?

- **Increase your ability to learn what others have to offer through the use of questions**

COMMUNICATION

13.5 Five Questioning Techniques

There are at least five different ways to draw out information, opinions, or ideas from team members in a facilitative manner. Try to include these techniques in your discussions with teammates to ensure you are understanding them clearly and prompting them effectively.

Technique	Purpose	Examples
1. Open-ended questions	• to open up a conversation • to encourage openness	"Why?" "How?" "When?" "Describe …" "Why do you think that's so?"
2. Clarification questions Pointer questions	• to make sure you understand • to draw out a specific point	"What do you mean by …?" "What other objectives do you have to …?" "I want to come back to something you said earlier …"
3. Prompting questions	• to encourage a hesitant speaker	"Can you say more about …?" "Go on."
4. Closed questions	• to limit a conversation • to find out specific information	Answered with a brief statement or "yes" or "no." "Do you favor the proposal?"
5. Leading questions	• to bring closure	"Do you agree that …?" "Since the data support it, do you think … ?"

I D E A

COMMUNICATION

13.6 The Rules of Listening

1. **Listen with *d'accord.*** Listen with your head and your heart so you will understand not just the facts being said, but the underlying emotion, intent, and meaning.

2. **Listen without prejudgment.** Listen with an open mind; otherwise, you're prejudiced, and conflict is almost guaranteed. Paraphrase, restate, and reflect with pure intent.

3. **Listen to learn.** By listening with an open mind, you might learn something you didn't know that might change your mind; you might learn something that will help you defend your position; you might learn that you and the speaker have more in common than you realized.

4. **Listen for agreement.** Even if you agree to disagree, that agreement can be more powerful than winning.

5. **Listen with flexibility.** Listen, realizing that even if what you hear causes you to change a belief, attitude, opinion, value, or behavior, you will have gained from the experience, not lost.

6. **Listen instead of waiting for your turn to talk.** Accord the speaker the same attention and respect that you would like other listeners to accord your words.

7. **Listen for the truth.** Listen to hear the truth of what is being said, and the truth will set you both free to do the right thing.

I D E A

• **Improve communication flow during team meetings**

COMMUNICATION

13.7 "Speaking Cards"

During team meetings, "speaking cards" are a way to keep communication flowing and the team focused on the topic at hand. If teams begin using the speaking cards effectively, they will find new habits created and, eventually, they will not need the cards.

TO USE SPEAKING CARDS

Team members flash the appropriate speaking card when they want to speak. The process observer or the team leader manages the process.

The Yellow Card Says:
> "I need clarification on what is being said."
> "I have something to add to what is being said."
> "I want to reinforce what is being said."

The Red Card Says:
> "I have something to add to what is being said."
> "I want to clarify something that is being said."
> "I want to reinforce something that is being said."
> "I have an idea related to what is being said."

The Green Card Says:
> "I have an idea that might take us off the topic, but it is important."
> "I have an opinion that I want to express."
> "I have a tangential idea that I need to voice."
> "I have an idea related to the topic, but not specifically regarding what is being said at the moment."

- Yellow Cards get top priority — in order flashed
- Red Cards speak next — in order flashed
- Green Cards speak after Yellow and Red Cards have finished
- Yellow Cards always get priority — even if flashed after the Red or Green Cards.

Materials needed: Three hand-sized cards (one yellow, one red, one green) per team member, cut from construction paper, cardboard, or card stock.

I D E A

WHAT'S IN IT FOR YOU?

• Become more aware of the communication patterns that exist on the team

COMMUNICATION

13.8 Communication Mapping

A communication map is a technique for observing who speaks and who doesn't, as well as who speaks to whom and how often. By observing the patterns of speaking and responding, dysfunctional communication can be identified and rectified.

TO CREATE A COMMUNICATION MAP

1. Draw a simple map with each team member identified.

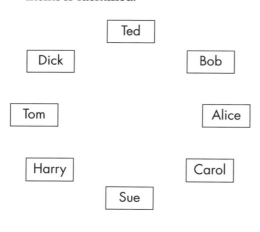

2. A line is drawn between the speaker and the team member being spoken to. If the speaker is making a general comment to the entire team — and indicating that through eye contact to all team members — then that, too, should be drawn.

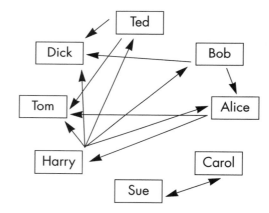

3. Notice emerging patterns. In the example above, Harry seems to be dominating the discussion. Depending on the topic or work being done, this may be appropriate. But consider the pattern with Sue and Carol. Their only comments seem to be side conversations, with no large group comments being made by them or to them.

I D E A

• **Encourage confidentiality as a communication technique that builds trust**

COMMUNICATION

13.9 Confidentiality

Most teams do not think about the issue of confidentiality until after something comes up that warrants a discussion. By then it is usually too late. Confidentiality involves the nondisclosure of information, opinions, team considerations, or discussions *outside* the team meetings, unless authorized by the team.

Confidentiality is an important communication norm to establish:

- Confidentiality establishes trust among team members that interpersonal issues that arise will not be inappropriately divulged to others.
- It ensures that sensitive organizational issues can be "shaped" by the team prior to their introduction to larger organizations.
- It assures the team and team members that ideas will *not* be taken out of context.
- It ensures that ideas in the brainstorming process will be just ideas for consideration. It creates a safer environment for true "blue sky thinking."

I D E A

- **Establish a system for identifying confidential issues and maintaining the team's trust**

COMMUNICATION

13.10 Confidentiality — Designating Red Flag Items

When team members feel they are discussing an organizationally sensitive topic or issue, they can designate it a red flag item. This red flag item would obligate each team member not to talk about the team's discussion concerning this topic outside the team meetings.

The minutes and agenda would have the initials *RF* before or after the specific item to remind each team member of the importance of confidentiality around that topic. The team should formulate some criteria for why an item might be designated a red flag item. Criteria might include personnel decisions, customer or competitor information, or technological secrets.

When team members get into interpersonal conflict and egos get out of hand, a very clear norm should be stated that holds that no description of those conflicts is to be talked about outside the meeting. No team member, whether one of the conflicting parties or just an observer, should discuss the conflict with a non-team member at any time.

While there may be exceptions on a case-by-case basis when this norm is in effect, more frank and open communication is possible.

IDEA

- **Develop the criteria to determine which issues are "red flagged" for confidentiality**

COMMUNICATION

13.11 Confidentiality — Criteria for Red Flag Items

There can be several reasons why an issue or problem should remain confidential and discussed only in team meetings. The team should brainstorm what those reasons might be. Here is a list you might use to get started:

- The competition might react before you can.
- The press may take the ideas or deliberations out of context before the ideas get a fair hearing.
- The organizational politics require that the status quo be diplomatically challenged and the team must do its preliminary work before the issue is fully aired.
- Team member reputations could be diminished if issues are openly discussed.
- A united team front, after alternatives have been considered, is required for organizational adoption.
- Team members not in attendance were discussed and need to be informed before discussions occur outside the meeting.
- Resistance to the team's purpose could be marshaled if certain issues were openly discussed.
- The price of outside resources could change if vendors knew the possible direction the team was taking.
- The net worth of the company assets could change given the team's deliberations.

CHAPTER FOURTEEN

DESIGNATED TEAM FEEDBACK

WHAT'S IN IT FOR YOU?

- Learn why it's important to formalize how and when feedback is given to team members
- Teach team members how to give and receive feedback
- Provide team members with the Designated Team Feedback worksheet to give timely and appropriate feedback

Feedback is the non-judgmental delivery of information about one's performance or behavior — or that's what it is supposed to be. Too often, however, feedback turns into dumping, blaming, or an emotional outpouring. Even more often, feedback is not given at all. As team leader, it is your responsibility to encourage thoughtful, constructive feedback between team members — not to be an intermediary or translator for others. This chapter will help you create a team environment that fosters forthright feedback and values honesty.

I D E A

DESIGNATED TEAM FEEDBACK

14.1 Why Formalize Feedback?

Designated team feedback is a process that encourages team members to give information about their perceptions of another team member's behavior. When feedback is given fairly and appropriately, all team members receive information about how their behavior affects others on the team.

Why this emphasis on a formal feedback process? The reasons for designated team feedback are as follows:

- Feedback allows team members to address interpersonal issues that arise in the course of the team's achieving its outcomes.
- A feedback process creates a safer environment for discussing interpersonal issues that might otherwise be left unsaid, but which affect relationships and productivity.
- The process opens up a problem-solving opportunity for team members to agree to make changes in their behavior in order to create more positive, helpful working relationships.

Feedback that is not given in an effective way can cause more damage than good. Consider these descriptions of poor feedback:

- Ineffective feedback that is ill-timed.
- Feedback that is evaluative, not descriptive.
- Feedback that criticizes behavior not within the person's control.
- Poor feedback that is general in nature, not about specific behaviors.
- Feedback given in a highly emotional tone, with animated facial expressions and quick, angular, nonverbal gestures.
- Feedback that is delivered as a threat and does not encourage positive change.
- Imposed feedback that is not requested or accepted.

I D E A

- **Teach team members how to deliver feedback constructively**

DESIGNATED TEAM FEEDBACK

14.2 Ten Guidelines for Giving Feedback

As team leader, it is important for you to teach team members how to give appropriate, constructive feedback — then hold them accountable for doing it. Remember, the best way to teach these skills is to model them.

Planning

1. Clarify your outcomes for the feedback. What behavior(s) would you like to see change?
2. Consider how you want the team member to behave, both during the feedback and after.
3. Try to foster a tone of helpfulness. Assume that the team member wants to be effective with you and others.
4. Try to give the feedback as soon as possible after the behavior has occurred. Given the reaction and receptivity of the team member, a specific time in the future could be set.

Giving the Feedback

5. Describe the team member's behavior and its effects on you. Make "I" statements and avoid "you" statements.
6. Give the team member a clear description of the desired behavior that will help you in the future.
7. Ask the team member to share his perceptions of his behavior, his intent, and his perceptions of the effect.
8. Try to reach agreement about the changes that need to be made.

Following Through

9. When, and if, the team member makes an effort to honor the change agreed upon, acknowledge those efforts.
10. If no change occurs, give the feedback again, being clear about the effects upon you if the behavior continues.

W O R K S H E E T

WHAT'S IN IT FOR YOU?

• Provide team members with a structured process for giving feedback

DESIGNATED TEAM FEEDBACK

14.3 Designated Team Feedback Worksheet

Name of team member to receive feedback: _____

Planning:

1. What behavior(s) would you like to see change?

   _____

   _____

2. How would you like to see this team member behave during the feedback? After?

   _____

   _____

Giving the feedback:

1. Describe the team member's disturbing behavior and how it affected you:

   _____

   _____

2. Describe the behavior you think would be more helpful to you:

   _____

   _____

Summarizing:

1. Record this team member's perception of his or her behavior, intent, and perceptions of the effect:

   _____

   _____

2. Summarize what has been agreed upon:

   _____

   _____

Date of the discussion: _____

I D E A

WHAT'S IN IT FOR YOU?

- **Teach team members to be prepared for how a receiver might react to getting feedback**

DESIGNATED TEAM FEEDBACK

14.4 When You Give, You Might Get Back

One of the reasons your team members may hesitate to deliver feedback is their fear of how it will be received. Feedback can strike team members differently depending upon the team, its norms and support, and the receiver's emotional state and self-concept — no matter how effectively the feedback is given.

You should help team members realize that there are many different possible reactions to their feedback, even if the feedback is positive in nature.

Positive feedback could produce the following responses:

- **Surprise.** In most teams, being caught "doing something right"* is an unusual occurrence. In a Protestant-work-ethic culture such as ours, praise is desirable, but not easily accepted.
- **Skepticism.** There is a tendency not to accept positive feedback without a slight wondering: "What does the giver really want?"
- **Acceptance.** The receiver realizes that another team member truly believes that a particular behavior is helpful and valuable.

Negative feedback could produce the following reactions:

- **Shock.** It is rare that behavior is openly confronted and described.
- **Disbelief.** There may be a reaction of questioning the appropriateness of the feedback. "Do they have the right person?"
- **Denial.** It may produce an immediate response of defensiveness; the giver's perceptions might be misinterpreted or considered incorrect or unfair.
- **Understanding.** There may come a moment in the receiver's mind when he or she begins to see the possible truth in the feedback and may see the impact on other team members.
- **Exploration.** If the team climate encourages growth, the receiver may reach the point of exploring the possible alternatives to his or her past behaviors.

---

*Ken Blanchard and Spencer Johnson, *The One Minute Manager* (New York: Morrow Press, 1981), p.39.

I D E A

• **Create a team norm that encourages team members to request feedback**

DESIGNATED TEAM FEEDBACK

14.5 Asking for Feedback

What if team members didn't wait for feedback, but actually asked for it? Imagine how much more accepting they would be of what they hear; imagine how much more forthcoming others would be to provide feedback.

At the beginning of each team meeting, ask team members these questions:

- Do you have a behavior you'd like to work on or improve during the course of the meeting? What is it specifically? (Example: "I want to improve my communication skills, especially paraphrasing.")
- How can other team members help you? (Example: "Point out when I respond to a person without making sure I understand him or her and clarifying what was said through paraphrasing.")
- Is there a particular team member you want to request help or feedback from? Who and why? (Example: "While I'd like feedback from anyone on the team, I would particularly appreciate getting feedback from Peter because we struggled to understand each other at the last meeting, and I think I can do better.")

At the end of the meeting, allow a few minutes during processing for team members to give each other the requested feedback — using Idea 14.2, "Ten Guidelines for Giving Feedback."

I D E A

- **Teach team members to receive feedback nondefensively**

DESIGNATED TEAM FEEDBACK

14.6 Guidelines for Receiving Feedback

Remind team members that they have a choice to behave differently as a result of the feedback they receive, but to do so they must understand the feedback and its benefits. A receiver must work to understand the issues or behaviors as seen through the eyes of the giver. Also remind those receiving feedback that the givers did not have to give the feedback; they could have withheld the information and made judgments without sharing their perceptions.

Provide your team with the following guidelines for receiving feedback nondefensively:

- Don't argue with another's perceptions — seek to understand them.
- Ask questions that clarify and allow for understanding. Ask: "How so?" "In what way?" "How often?" "When?" "How did that affect you?" "Can you be more specific?"
- Project an open-minded approach by asking the giver for suggestions concerning behaviors that may be more helpful.
- Check for understanding by repeating what you heard and asking for confirmation from the giver.
- Thank the giver for the feedback. Remind yourself and the giver that in many instances, giving feedback can be as difficult as receiving feedback.

I D E A

- **Stop malicious gossip, backstabbing, and indirect communication that, over time, can destroy a team**

DESIGNATED TEAM FEEDBACK

14.7 If You're Invited to a Third Party, Don't Go

It may take two to tango, but it takes three to destroy the dance. When two people do not share their concerns, dislikes, or problems with each other, but address issues to a third party, they begin to sabotage the trust and honesty that a HIT requires.

The fastest way to eliminate destructive third-party behavior is to establish a norm that says:

> **"I will not be a third party to feedback that someone else should be hearing directly."**

Of course, you should still encourage all team members to agree to the following norm:

> **"I will never talk about a team member to another (team member or non-team member) if I haven't already addressed it with the team member first."**

One organization actually had team members sign an agreement to the effect that they would simply not listen to feedback meant for someone else. People committed to a behavior something like this:

> **Terry approaches you and says, "I'm really irritated with what Bob said in our last meeting. ..."**
>
> **You respond, "You know, Terry, I feel very uncomfortable talking about Bob without him here to defend himself. Why don't I ring him and see if he can join us?"**

Explain to team members that if another team member complains to them, accuses, or belittles another team member, their response should be

> **"Have you shared your feelings with this person?"**

If it has not been shared, encourage the complaining person to do so.

Create a team axiom:

> **Responsible team members "confront with care," not "complain in comfort."**

CHAPTER FIFTEEN

LEADERSHIP IN HITs

WHAT'S IN IT FOR YOU?

• Clarify the role, importance, and characteristics of the team leader
• Further clarify the sponsor's role in leadership
• Encourage emerging leadership from the ranks of the team

L eadership is one of the most elusive of skills. Countless books have been written on the subject, including this one. This particular chapter succinctly captures the most basic elements of what it means to be the leader of a team.

I D E A

• **Understand why leadership is so important for HITs**

LEADERSHIP IN HITs

15.1 Orchestrating a HIT

Leadership in teams is often misunderstood. The team leader must select the music, arrange it, and orchestrate it, *but cannot play it*. To create a HIT, the leader must understand and have such a deep passion for the music that he or she creates the setting in which it can come into being.

Whether you are referring to an athletic, school, or community group or a work team, one leader rarely dominates a high-performing team. Whether you are the designated leader of a team, or you are responsible for recruiting or forming a team, you must be careful. Capable leaders of teams must be able to focus team members on a collective purpose, but be willing to give their power away!

Leadership is important to HITs for the following reasons:

- There must be leadership for work to be accomplished collectively.
- Leadership of effective teams does not fall on one person.
- Lack of leadership skills will severely limit a team's capacity.
- Being a boss of the group and being a team leader are different roles.
- Being a team leader requires flexibility in behavior.

Despite good intentions and talent, leadership may be ineffective in the following situations:

- The team's purpose and outcomes cannot be made clear.
- Individual team members cannot become committed to the purpose of the team.
- The leader's own needs result in domination or control of the team.
- The team charter continually changes.
- Team membership continually changes.
- The organization that chartered the team holds the appointed leader accountable, but not the team.
- The organizational incentives are for individual performance, not team performance.

IDEA

WHAT'S IN IT FOR YOU?

- **Raise awareness of some general "truths" about team leadership**

LEADERSHIP IN HITs

15.2 Seven Considerations for an Appointed or Emerging Team Leader

1. An effective team leader is a "first among equals" and will most likely emerge through both technical knowledge *and* interpersonal skills.
2. Different members should become leaders for different work processes, different phases of the work, or different issues that face the group.
3. An effective team leader must make decisions or facilitate team decisions without infringing on the perceived autonomy of other team members.
4. As the team matures and progresses, effective team leadership has more to do with facilitating than with exercising control.
5. An effective team leader views the main leadership function as helping to focus the group's attention on a vision and the aspirations for that vision.
6. Most teams fail not because of a lack or improper use of technical knowledge, but because of a lack or improper use of the group interaction skills that need to be structured initially by the team leadership.
7. In the case of an appointed leader, the team may want to select its "own" leaders once consensus has been reached about the team charter.

I D E A

- Guide the team sponsor by understanding some general "truths" about sponsorship

LEADERSHIP IN HITs

15.3 Six Considerations for the Nonmember Sponsor

Even though the sponsor may have chartered the team and selected the team members, you may have to ensure that the sponsor strives to do the following:

1. Keep the massive stress the team can feel in check by buffering bureaucratic interference.
2. Try to assure that the team will not be dominated by one individual.
3. Keep his or her interventions to a minimum.
4. After clearly chartering the team, never intervene until the team has requested help.
5. After clearly chartering the team, intervene only after the team has learned through its struggle and completed its task and seeks approval or validation.
6. Never give in to the idea that his or her power is more important than the talent that has been assembled on the team.

I D E A

WHAT'S IN IT FOR YOU?

• Begin building skills in team members that will enable leadership eventually to be shared

LEADERSHIP IN HITs

15.4 Six Strategies for Creating Emerging Leadership

1. Rotate the responsibility for chairing a meeting among all team members, but make sure they chair more than one meeting in a row, so that leadership skills and momentum can be cultivated.
2. Ask various team members to represent the team's progress and outcomes to "outside" groups during the period of the team's activity.
3. Ask various team members to act as consultants or experts to newly forming teams.
4. Ask team members to take the lead in subgroups of the team that are responsible for components of the group's work.
5. Ask various team members to analyze the team's process and work interaction, at the end of meetings.
6. Train all team members on group development skills, group process skills, team meeting skills, and interpersonal skills.

CHAPTER SIXTEEN

TEAM TRAINING

WHAT'S IN IT FOR YOU?

- Answer questions to help you identify the kind of training your team needs
- Determine the sequence, timing, and delivery of training
- Consider a variety of resources for continued training

This chapter focuses team training on "soft skills," those hard-to-do, vital behaviors that all team members need at their disposal if they are going to be contributing members of the team.

I D E A

TEAM TRAINING

16.1 To Train or Not to Train — These Are the Questions

There are two general areas to consider for training your team. The first is *technical training,* which upgrades skills around the problem or product in which the team is involved. Technical training is dependent upon team composition and product outcomes, but is obviously very important. Upgrading technical skills may not be appropriate for all team members, however.

The second type of training is *team training,* which increases the team members' skills in the process of teaming. We will focus on team-training experiences that help guide, direct, or support the team's ability to function better as a team. The kinds of skills or insights learned through team training are considered "soft skills," and as a result are often not taken seriously. But, as it has been said, "The hard stuff is easy, it's the soft stuff that's hard."

Team training involves secondary issues, such as costs, means, duration, and logistics, but answers to the following five questions must be thought through carefully before the secondary issues can be appropriately addressed. Ideas 16.2 through 16.7 can help you gain perspective on these central questions.

1. What kind of training should team members receive?
2. What kind of training should the team leader receive?
3. When should the team members receive training?
4. Should team training occur as a team or as individuals?
5. Where could the team leader start to find resources needed for training?

I D E A

WHAT'S IN IT FOR YOU?

• Create a variety of experiences that perform the function of "training"

TEAM TRAINING

16.2 What Is Training?

When you think of the term *training*, you should first think of formal classroom experiences. However, we believe training really involves any experience that results in the transfer of information, data, or skill.

Training could take the form of experiences such as the following:

- Visiting a site to observe a technique or process in operation
- Using a consultant to process a team meeting
- Requiring all team members to read and discuss a specific book
- All team members attending a workshop on problem solving
- Viewing a video that will be further discussed by the team
- Interviewing a prospective customer or user of the team's output
- Reviewing feedback from team members about your team behavior
- Engaging in a simulation or game that encourages learning by lowering the stakes, yet approximates the real circumstances
- Experiencing various team meetings and reflecting on how the meetings could be improved
- Developing and finalizing a team charter.

While all these experiences can be considered training, we advocate that certain workshop and classroom experiences be conducted for your team.

IDEA

• **Examine the areas you may consider for team training**

TEAM TRAINING

16.3 What Kind of Training Should Team Members Receive?

There are nine key skill areas needed by team members for effective team participation:

1. Conflict resolution techniques
2. Decision-making strategies
3. Communication
4. Giving and receiving feedback
5. Understanding the behavior patterns of yourself and others
6. Understanding phases of team evolution
7. Meeting structure
8. Charter development
9. Problem-solving techniques

Of course, there are other topics, but none are as central to team process as the ones listed above. We recommend that training on these topics be strongly considered for all team members.

I D E A

- **Evaluate your own training needs**

TEAM TRAINING

16.4 What Kind of Training Should the Team Leader Receive?

The type of training that the team leader and team members receive should differ very little. Both the leader and team members need to be skillful in all team processes, such as problem solving and conflict resolution. As team leader, you may need less technical knowledge than individual team members; however, all members need process skills.

The sequence of team leader training is, of course, different. You should have prior awareness and skill in team process. Timing is everything in life, and team leader training is no exception. The skill areas discussed in this book are only a start. It is hoped that you have at least had past experience as a team member on a productive team. At a minimum, you should observe a productive team at work.

We recommend that any prospective team leader have some skill-building training before the chartering process has been started with team members.

IDEA

• **Determine a sequence and timing for team training**

TEAM TRAINING

16.5   When Should Team Members Receive Training?

	Type of Training	Delivery Method
Unit A	Problem-solving techniques	Workshop
	Conflict resolution techniques	Workshop
	Decision-making strategies	Workshop
	Communication techniques	Workshop
Unit B	Charter development	Practical Experience
	Meeting structure	Practical Experience
Unit C	Understanding behavior patterns	Workshop + Practical experience
	Understanding phases of team evolution	Workshop + Practical experience
	Giving and receiving feedback	Workshop + Practical experience

The knowledge learned in Unit A in the areas of problem solving, conflict resolution, decision making, and communication is more than helpful as team members formulate the team's operating guidelines and norms during the chartering process. Therefore, Unit A skills should be taught *before* the chartering process.

The training in Unit B is the experience of the group members as they work together to create the team charter. The aid of an outside expert should be considered if the team leader is not proficient at leading the chartering process.

Unit C is more appropriate for discussion and development after some team meetings have occurred and there is "real" experience on which to draw for learning. After the team has been meeting for a while, the patterns, phases, and feedback become more relevant.

I D E A

- **Consider which skills are best taught to the intact team and which can be taught to individuals apart from the team**

TEAM TRAINING

16.6 Training as a Team or as an Individual?

The skills needed for the team to efficiently begin the chartering process and create group norms and guidelines (Unit A training, Idea 16.5) are best suited to a workshop delivery. These skills can be imparted on an individual basis with group members attending different workshops independently, but all members should have the same basic skills for the team's start-up time to be reduced.

Team development and skill development actually need to start during the creation of the charter. The charter and meeting structure skills should be done as an intact team.

Skill building around topics such as behavioral patterns, phases of team evolution, and feedback could be done individually, but the team would be best served by training team members as a group.

I D E A

TEAM TRAINING

16.7 Team Training Resources

While the world is just waiting to sell its services to you, consider the following ideas:

- Contact your local college or university's continuing education division for references.
- Contact your local chapter of the American Society of Trainers and Developers (ASTD) for references.
- Use the ads in training magazines for references.
- Ask contacts from other companies for recommendations.
- Contact authors of books you liked on the topic.
- Call us.

CHAPTER SEVENTEEN

ASSESSING TEAM PROCESS

WHAT'S IN IT FOR YOU?

- Develop team members into participant observers who proactively comply with operating guidelines and norms
- Use assessment checklists to evaluate and discuss perceptions of behavior of team members relating to guidelines and norms
- Use assessment checklists to evaluate your team's structure and current temperature

If your team is already up and running, this chapter might be one that you want to focus your attention on initially. You will find an assortment of checklists to gauge the effectiveness of your meetings and their structure, problem solving, decision making, conflict resolution, communication, feedback, leadership, participation, roles, responsibilities, goals, and celebrations. Finally, there's a checklist to see how close your team is to being considered a HIT.

I D E A

- Learn the importance of understanding what is happening in your team from a process as well as product viewpoint

ASSESSING TEAM PROCESS

17.1 Why Bother to Assess?

By gauging how the team feels about the group's problem solving, conflict resolution, decision making, team meeting structure, communication, and feedback, team members can improve *how* they do their work — which will translate into improving *what* they do. Process improvement will generally mean better team outcomes or products. You need to evaluate how effective the team processes are to get an idea of which processes need improvement. Use the worksheets in this chapter to collect team member perceptions concerning group processes. Oftentimes, just asking team members for input improves the quality of working together.

By helping your team members to assess their process, you can accomplish the following:
- Reduce tension among team members by allowing a safe mechanism for venting feelings.
- Increase team output because members become aware of behaviors that could or should be improved during evaluation.
- Decrease the amount of time it takes for the group to do its work because a better process results in greater efficiency.
- Involve all team members in examination of the team process, thus getting buy-in when changes are required.

Assessing the team's process could prove ineffective under the following conditions:
- The team leader dominates the group.
- There are no sanctions for team members who act outside the team norm.
- There is a history of assessment that results in no change.

I D E A

- **Explain to your team members the important difference between a process observer and a participant observer in the ongoing assessment of team process**

ASSESSING TEAM PROCESS

17.2 Participant Observers

Every team has process observers. These people are easy to recognize because, after the meeting, they are in the halls talking about what they observed. They noticed how decisions were reached, how people did or didn't handle conflict, or why the meeting was good or bad. A process observer is a person who *watches* the work that is accomplished, as well as how the group goes about getting the work done.

Likewise, every team needs participant observers. A *participant observer* is someone who not only watches the team's process, but also helps work on task issues. A participant observer is in the thick of things, yet he or she is able to stand back and analyze team dynamics.

Every team needs a designated process observer. Every team member needs to be a participant observer.

Participant observers are important for the following reasons:
- All team members must take responsibility for the way the team does its work (process), to keep the norms sharp and appropriate.
- All team members must participate in the work of the team in order for the team to capitalize on everyone's expertise.
- Being an observer without being a participant means the team member has dropped out of the work of the group.
- Failure to be an observer could lead to poor process, strained interpersonal relationships, and poor team outcomes.

When is being a participant observer ineffective? *Never.* Being a participant observer is the essence of "teamness."

I D E A

ASSESSING TEAM PROCESS

17.3 Using Assessment Checklists

On the following pages you will find a number of checklists that you can use to stimulate dialogue with your team. Follow these guidelines for using the checklists:

- Duplicate enough for each team member.
- Do not use more than one or two checklists in one meeting.
- Use the checklists to evaluate one or two meetings at a time, rather than evaluating many meetings over time.
- Next to the questions that generated the discussion, make notes of the behaviors that typify the rating on the checklist.
- Once the checklists have been completed by all team members, starting with the first question, ask team members to share their ratings.
- When wide disparities exist among team members, ask those with the widest differences in numbers to share the instances in team behavior that led them to their conclusions.
- The idea is *not* to get people to change their ratings. The objective is to understand the behaviors, seen by most, that result in agreement about the status of the group's process.
- Collect and keep the checklists. Date them and consider using them for future comparison if the process topic is ever reassessed.

W O R K S H E E T

WHAT'S IN IT FOR YOU?

• Evaluate and discuss perceptions of your team meetings

ASSESSING TEAM PROCESS

17.4 Meeting Evaluation Checklist

Circle the number that best represents your perceptions of the meeting.*

1. Were the goals of the meeting clear?

1	2	3	4	5	6	7	8	9	10
Yes				Somewhat					No

Behavior used to judge: _____

_____

2. Was the role of team member made clear?

1	2	3	4	5	6	7	8	9	10
Yes				Somewhat					No

Behavior used to judge: _____

_____

3. Did the group stay on task?

1	2	3	4	5	6	7	8	9	10
Yes				Somewhat					No

Behavior used to judge: _____

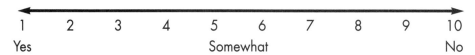

_____

4. Were the stated goals of the meeting accomplished?

1	2	3	4	5	6	7	8	9	10
Yes				Somewhat					No

Behavior used to judge: _____

_____

5. Were assignments made for clear action items?

1	2	3	4	5	6	7	8	9	10
Yes				Somewhat					No

Behavior used to judge: _____

_____

6. Was the decision-making process followed?

1	2	3	4	5	6	7	8	9	10
Yes				Somewhat					No

Behavior used to judge: _____

_____

7. Were you satisfied with the meeting?

1	2	3	4	5	6	7	8	9	10
Yes				Somewhat					No

Behavior used to judge: _____

_____

*See Ideas 9.1–9.16, "Meeting Structure," for elaboration.

W O R K S H E E T

WHAT'S IN IT FOR YOU?

- **Evaluate the effectiveness of your team's meeting structure with your team members**

ASSESSING TEAM PROCESS

17.5 Meeting Structure Evaluation Checklist

Circle the number that best represents your perceptions of the meeting structure.*

1. Are the agendas prepared for team meetings ahead of time?

1	2	3	4	5	6	7	8	9	10
Yes				Somewhat					No

Behavior used to judge: _____

_____

2. Is it easy for team members to place items on the agenda?

1	2	3	4	5	6	7	8	9	10
Yes				Somewhat					No

Behavior used to judge: _____

_____

3. Are all the ideas discussed in team meetings recorded?

1	2	3	4	5	6	7	8	9	10
Yes				Somewhat					No

Behavior used to judge: _____

_____

4. Are the minutes helpful to orient and document team activities?

```
1     2     3     4     5     6     7     8     9     10
Yes                     Somewhat                      No
```

Behavior used to judge: _____

_____

5. Do team members read the prepared materials before coming to team meetings?

```
1     2     3     4     5     6     7     8     9     10
Yes                     Somewhat                      No
```

Behavior used to judge: _____

_____

6. Does a team member visibly record team ideas while discussion is going on?

```
1     2     3     4     5     6     7     8     9     10
Yes                     Somewhat                      No
```

Behavior used to judge: _____

_____

7. Do team members understand the criteria used for including an item on the agenda?

```
1     2     3     4     5     6     7     8     9     10
Yes                     Somewhat                      No
```

Behavior used to judge: _____

_____

8. As an individual team member, are you satisfied with the structure used in your team meetings?

```
1     2     3     4     5     6     7     8     9     10
Yes                     Somewhat                      No
```

Behavior used to judge: _____

_____

*See Ideas 9.1–9.16, "Meeting Structure," for elaboration.

W O R K S H E E T

WHAT'S IN IT FOR YOU?

• **Evaluate and discuss the effectiveness of the team's problem-solving process**

ASSESSING TEAM PROCESS

17.6 Problem Solving Evaluation Checklist

Circle the number that best represents your perceptions of the team's problem-solving process.*

1. Do participants clearly define the problems being discussed?

1	2	3	4	5	6	7	8	9	10
Yes				Somewhat					No

Behavior used to judge: _____

_____

2. Are several alternatives considered?

1	2	3	4	5	6	7	8	9	10
Yes				Somewhat					No

Behavior used to judge: _____

_____

3. Are the pros and cons of each alternative examined?

1	2	3	4	5	6	7	8	9	10
Yes				Somewhat					No

Behavior used to judge: _____

_____

4. Does the team follow a systematic approach to problem solving?

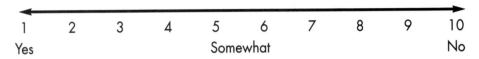

1	2	3	4	5	6	7	8	9	10
Yes				Somewhat					No

Behavior used to judge: _____

_____

5. Do participants consider new solutions as well as time-tested ones?

1	2	3	4	5	6	7	8	9	10
Yes				Somewhat					No

Behavior used to judge: _____

_____

6. Does the group follow the rules of brainstorming?

1	2	3	4	5	6	7	8	9	10
Yes				Somewhat					No

Behavior used to judge: _____

_____

7. Does the group take the necessary time to reach good solutions?

1	2	3	4	5	6	7	8	9	10
Yes				Somewhat					No

Behavior used to judge: _____

_____

8. As an individual team member, are you satisfied with the way the team is solving problems?

1	2	3	4	5	6	7	8	9	10
Yes				Somewhat					No

Behavior used to judge: _____

_____

*See Ideas 10.1–10.17, "Problem Solving," for elaboration.

W O R K S H E E T

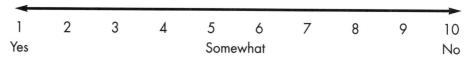

WHAT'S IN IT FOR YOU?

• **Evaluate and discuss your team's decision-making process**

ASSESSING TEAM PROCESS

17.7 Decision Making Evaluation Checklist

Circle the number that best represents your perceptions of the team's decision-making process.*

1. Did the group designate how the team would make decisions?

1	2	3	4	5	6	7	8	9	10
Yes				Somewhat					No

Behavior used to judge: _____

_____

2. Did team members accept the approach?

1	2	3	4	5	6	7	8	9	10
Yes				Somewhat					No

Behavior used to judge: _____

_____

3. Were all available resources used to make the decision?

1	2	3	4	5	6	7	8	9	10
Yes				Somewhat					No

Behavior used to judge: _____

_____

4. Is the decision-making process used producing the best decisions?

```
←——————————————————————————————————→
1    2    3    4    5    6    7    8    9    10
Yes                 Somewhat                  No
```

Behavior used to judge: _____

_____

5. Are clear decisions being made?

```
←——————————————————————————————————→
1    2    3    4    5    6    7    8    9    10
Yes                 Somewhat                  No
```

Behavior used to judge: _____

_____

6. Do any important issues go undecided?

```
←——————————————————————————————————→
1    2    3    4    5    6    7    8    9    10
Yes                 Somewhat                  No
```

Behavior used to judge: _____

_____

7. Does any team member make contributions that do not receive any kind of response?

```
←——————————————————————————————————→
1    2    3    4    5    6    7    8    9    10
Yes                 Somewhat                  No
```

Behavior used to judge: _____

_____

8. As a team member, are you satisfied with the way the team is making decisions?

```
←——————————————————————————————————→
1    2    3    4    5    6    7    8    9    10
Yes                 Somewhat                  No
```

Behavior used to judge: _____

_____

*See Ideas 11.1–11.7, "Decision-Making Strategies," for elaboration.

W O R K S H E E T

WHAT'S IN IT FOR YOU?

• **Evaluate and discuss the effectiveness of the conflict resolution strategies used in your team**

ASSESSING TEAM PROCESS

17.8 Conflict Resolution Evaluation Checklist

Circle the number that best represents your perceptions of the conflict resolution practices used by the team.*

1. Do team members speak their minds even if it means creating conflict?

1	2	3	4	5	6	7	8	9	10
Yes				Somewhat					No

Behavior used to judge: _____

_____

2. Do conflicts that have arisen stimulate creative solutions?

1	2	3	4	5	6	7	8	9	10
Yes				Somewhat					No

Behavior used to judge: _____

_____

3. Do other team members help those who are in conflict?

1	2	3	4	5	6	7	8	9	10
Yes				Somewhat					No

Behavior used to judge: _____

_____

4. Do team members avoid conflict?

1	2	3	4	5	6	7	8	9	10
Yes				Somewhat					No

Behavior used to judge: _____

_____

5. Are the conflicts between team members value-based?

1	2	3	4	5	6	7	8	9	10
Yes				Somewhat					No

Behavior used to judge: _____

_____

6. Do team members use collaboration as a strategy to resolve conflict?

1	2	3	4	5	6	7	8	9	10
Yes				Somewhat					No

Behavior used to judge: _____

_____

7. Does the team use a systematic approach to resolving conflict between team members?

1	2	3	4	5	6	7	8	9	10
Yes				Somewhat					No

Behavior used to judge: _____

_____

8. As an individual team member, are you satisfied with the way conflicts are resolved in the team?

1	2	3	4	5	6	7	8	9	10
Yes				Somewhat					No

Behavior used to judge: _____

_____

*See Ideas 12.1–12.14, "Conflict Resolution Strategies," for elaboration.

WORKSHEET

WHAT'S IN IT FOR YOU?

- Evaluate and discuss how effective the communication is among your team members

ASSESSING TEAM PROCESS

17.9   Communication Evaluation Checklist

Circle the number that best represents your perceptions of the way team members communicate with each other.*

1. Do team members paraphrase and summarize what others have said?

1	2	3	4	5	6	7	8	9	10
Yes				Somewhat					No

Behavior used to judge: _____

_____

2. Do team members acknowledge the feelings expressed in team meetings?

1	2	3	4	5	6	7	8	9	10
Yes				Somewhat					No

Behavior used to judge: _____

_____

3. Do team members show appropriate, respectful nonverbal behavior to each other?

1	2	3	4	5	6	7	8	9	10
Yes				Somewhat					No

Behavior used to judge: _____

_____

4. Do team members ask open-ended questions that are truly open-ended?

1	2	3	4	5	6	7	8	9	10
Yes				Somewhat					No

Behavior used to judge: _____

_____

5. Do team members, when so designated, keep discussions confidential?

1	2	3	4	5	6	7	8	9	10
Yes				Somewhat					No

Behavior used to judge: _____

_____

6. Do team members call attention to those who do not listen?

1	2	3	4	5	6	7	8	9	10
Yes				Somewhat					No

Behavior used to judge: _____

_____

7. Do team members listen with open minds to the ideas of others?

1	2	3	4	5	6	7	8	9	10
Yes				Somewhat					No

Behavior used to judge: _____

_____

8. As an individual team member, are you satisfied with the way team members communicate with each other?

1	2	3	4	5	6	7	8	9	10
Yes				Somewhat					No

Behavior used to judge: _____

_____

*See Ideas 13.1–13.11, "Communication," for elaboration.

W O R K S H E E T

WHAT'S IN IT FOR YOU?

- **Evaluate and discuss the effectiveness of feedback procedures used in your team**

ASSESSING TEAM PROCESS

17.10 Feedback Evaluation Checklist

Circle the number that best represents your perceptions of the way team members give and receive feedback.*

1. Do team members give feedback directly and clearly to others?

1	2	3	4	5	6	7	8	9	10
Yes				Somewhat					No

Behavior used to judge: _____

_____

2. Do team members check for understanding after the feedback has been given?

1	2	3	4	5	6	7	8	9	10
Yes				Somewhat					No

Behavior used to judge: _____

_____

3. Do team members give feedback in a tone of helpfulness?

1	2	3	4	5	6	7	8	9	10
Yes				Somewhat					No

Behavior used to judge: _____

_____

4. Do team members describe specific behaviors that can be changed when giving feedback?

1	2	3	4	5	6	7	8	9	10
Yes				Somewhat					No

Behavior used to judge: _____

_____

5. Do team members time their feedback appropriately?

1	2	3	4	5	6	7	8	9	10
Yes				Somewhat					No

Behavior used to judge: _____

_____

6. Do team members acknowledge the efforts of a team member who changes behavior as a result of feedback?

1	2	3	4	5	6	7	8	9	10
Yes				Somewhat					No

Behavior used to judge: _____

_____

7. Do team members value the feedback they receive from others?

1	2	3	4	5	6	7	8	9	10
Yes				Somewhat					No

Behavior used to judge: _____

_____

8. As an individual team member, are you satisfied with the way team members give and receive feedback?

1	2	3	4	5	6	7	8	9	10
Yes				Somewhat					No

Behavior used to judge: _____

_____

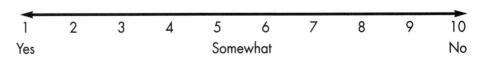

*See Ideas 14.1–14.7, "Designated Team Feedback," for elaboration.

WORKSHEET

WHAT'S IN IT FOR YOU?

• Evaluate and discuss the way leadership is exercised in your team

ASSESSING TEAM PROCESS

17.11 Leadership Evaluation Checklist

Circle the number that best represents your perceptions of the way leadership is exercised in the team.*

1. Do team members defer to one person in the group?

1	2	3	4	5	6	7	8	9	10
Yes				Somewhat					No

Behavior used to judge: _____

_____

2. Does leadership emerge based upon competence and commitment to the goals of the team?

1	2	3	4	5	6	7	8	9	10
Yes				Somewhat					No

Behavior used to judge: _____

_____

3. Does the appointed or hierarchical leader give up the decision-making prerogative to the team?

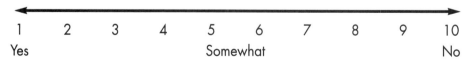

1	2	3	4	5	6	7	8	9	10
Yes				Somewhat					No

Behavior used to judge: _____

_____

4. Does leadership emerge to facilitate the team's process?

1	2	3	4	5	6	7	8	9	10
Yes				Somewhat					No

Behavior used to judge: _____

_____

5. Does the team leader show leadership without infringing on the autonomy of other team members?

1	2	3	4	5	6	7	8	9	10
Yes				Somewhat					No

Behavior used to judge: _____

_____

6. Did the sponsor of the team charter the team effectively?

1	2	3	4	5	6	7	8	9	10
Yes				Somewhat					No

Behavior used to judge: _____

_____

7. Do various team members represent the team to outside groups?

1	2	3	4	5	6	7	8	9	10
Yes				Somewhat					No

Behavior used to judge: _____

_____

8. As an individual team member, are you satisfied with how leadership is exercised in this team?

1	2	3	4	5	6	7	8	9	10
Yes				Somewhat					No

Behavior used to judge: _____

_____

*See Ideas 15.1–15.4, "Leadership in HITs," for elaboration.

W O R K S H E E T

WHAT'S IN IT FOR YOU?

• **Evaluate and discuss the participation patterns of members on your team**

ASSESSING TEAM PROCESS

17.12 Participation Evaluation Checklist

Circle the number that best represents your perceptions of the participation patterns on the team.

1. Is anyone seen as "outside" the team?

1	2	3	4	5	6	7	8	9	10
Yes				Somewhat					No

Behavior used to judge: _____

_____

2. Do some members move in and out of the team?

1	2	3	4	5	6	7	8	9	10
Yes				Somewhat					No

Behavior used to judge: _____

_____

3. Are there low vs. high participators?

1	2	3	4	5	6	7	8	9	10
Yes				Somewhat					No

Behavior used to judge: _____

_____

4. Do people "talk down" to each other?

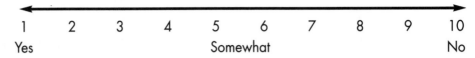

1	2	3	4	5	6	7	8	9	10
Yes				Somewhat					No

Behavior used to judge: _____

_____

5. Do people have high vs. low influence with the team?

1	2	3	4	5	6	7	8	9	10
Yes				Somewhat					No

Behavior used to judge: _____

_____

6. Is there a struggle for leadership among team members?

1	2	3	4	5	6	7	8	9	10
Yes				Somewhat					No

Behavior used to judge: _____

_____

7. If people are silent, are they drawn out?

1	2	3	4	5	6	7	8	9	10
Yes				Somewhat					No

Behavior used to judge: _____

_____

8. Are you satisfied with the way participation is handled in the team?

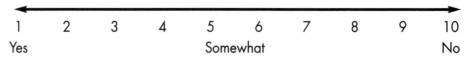

1	2	3	4	5	6	7	8	9	10
Yes				Somewhat					No

Behavior used to judge: _____

_____

W O R K S H E E T

WHAT'S IN IT FOR YOU?

- **Evaluate and discuss the way roles and responsibilities are handled on the team**

ASSESSING TEAM PROCESS

17.13 Roles and Responsibilities Evaluation Checklist

Circle the number that best represents your perceptions of how roles and responsibilities are dealt with on the team.

1. Are the roles and responsibilities clearly defined for each member?

1	2	3	4	5	6	7	8	9	10
Yes				Somewhat					No

Behavior used to judge: _____

_____

2. Are the areas of responsibility that must be shared with other outside groups clearly identified?

1	2	3	4	5	6	7	8	9	10
Yes				Somewhat					No

Behavior used to judge: _____

_____

3. Are the roles and responsibilities appropriate (necessary and sufficient) to meet the team's goals?

1	2	3	4	5	6	7	8	9	10
Yes				Somewhat					No

Behavior used to judge: _____

_____

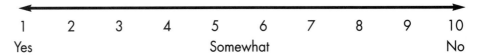

4. Are team members competent to fulfill their roles and responsibilities?

1	2	3	4	5	6	7	8	9	10
Yes				Somewhat					No

Behavior used to judge: _____

_____

5. Do team members help to train each other on the roles and responsibilities whenever possible?

1	2	3	4	5	6	7	8	9	10
Yes				Somewhat					No

Behavior used to judge: _____

_____

6. Are members fully committed to fulfilling their roles and responsibilities?

1	2	3	4	5	6	7	8	9	10
Yes				Somewhat					No

Behavior used to judge: _____

_____

7. Is the leadership role and responsibility shared among team members?

1	2	3	4	5	6	7	8	9	10
Yes				Somewhat					No

Behavior used to judge: _____

_____

8. Are you satisfied with the way the team handles the roles and responsibilities of this team?

1	2	3	4	5	6	7	8	9	10
Yes				Somewhat					No

Behavior used to judge: _____

_____

W O R K S H E E T

WHAT'S IN IT FOR YOU?

- **Evaluate and discuss the clarity of the team's goals and results**

ASSESSING TEAM PROCESS

17.14 Goals and Results Evaluation Checklist

Circle the number that best represents your perceptions of the clarity of the team's goals and results.

1. Do all team members clearly understand the outcomes for the team's work?

1	2	3	4	5	6	7	8	9	10
Yes				Somewhat					No

Behavior used to judge: _____

_____

2. Are the implications for action spelled out clearly?

1	2	3	4	5	6	7	8	9	10
Yes				Somewhat					No

Behavior used to judge: _____

_____

3. Do the team outcomes meet the customers' needs?

1	2	3	4	5	6	7	8	9	10
Yes				Somewhat					No

Behavior used to judge: _____

_____

4. Are the team members satisfied with the proposed team outcomes?

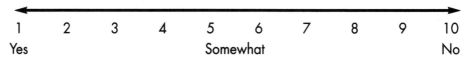

1	2	3	4	5	6	7	8	9	10
Yes				Somewhat					No

Behavior used to judge: _____

_____

5. Are the team goals aligned with those of the larger organization?

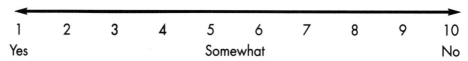

1	2	3	4	5	6	7	8	9	10
Yes				Somewhat					No

Behavior used to judge: _____

_____

6. Can the **team goals** or outcomes be supported by available resources?

1	2	3	4	5	6	7	8	9	10
Yes				Somewhat					No

Behavior used to judge: _____

_____

7. Do the team members regard team goals as motivating and fair?

1	2	3	4	5	6	7	8	9	10
Yes				Somewhat					No

Behavior used to judge: _____

_____

8. Are you satisfied with the way the team handles goal setting?

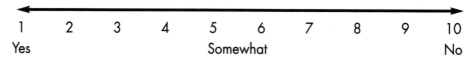

1	2	3	4	5	6	7	8	9	10
Yes				Somewhat					No

Behavior used to judge: _____

_____

W O R K S H E E T

WHAT'S IN IT FOR YOU?

• **Judge with team members if your team is a HIT**

ASSESSING TEAM PROCESS

17.15 High Impact Team Evaluation Checklist

Circle the number that best represents your perceptions of the way the team operates.

1. Do all team members clearly understand the outcomes of the team?

1	2	3	4	5	6	7	8	9	10
Yes				Somewhat					No

Behavior used to judge: _____

_____

2. Are all team members participating and invested in achieving the team's outcomes?

1	2	3	4	5	6	7	8	9	10
Yes				Somewhat					No

Behavior used to judge: _____

_____

3. Do all team members actively listen to each other?

1	2	3	4	5	6	7	8	9	10
Yes				Somewhat					No

Behavior used to judge: _____

_____

4. Do team members make their opposition known rather than sabotage the consensus?

1	2	3	4	5	6	7	8	9	10
Yes				Somewhat					No

Behavior used to judge: _____

_____

5. Do team members give feedback to each other frequently, directly, and in the spirit of helpfulness?

1	2	3	4	5	6	7	8	9	10
Yes				Somewhat					No

Behavior used to judge: _____

_____

6. Do team members make and keep commitments when producing work for the team?

1	2	3	4	5	6	7	8	9	10
Yes				Somewhat					No

Behavior used to judge: _____

_____

7. Does leadership of the team shift over time, depending upon the issues?

1	2	3	4	5	6	7	8	9	10
Yes				Somewhat					No

Behavior used to judge: _____

_____

8. Do team members, when group processes have been violated, call attention to it and help team members deal with it?

1	2	3	4	5	6	7	8	9	10
Yes				Somewhat					No

Behavior used to judge: _____

_____

SECTION 3

SUSTAINING IDEAS: REJUVENATING OR ENDING A TEAM'S WORK

This section provides you, the team leader, with the insights and knowledge to elevate a good team to a mega-HIT.

Despite the attention to the technical aspects of what your team is doing, it is almost always the people problems that will make or break a team. Chapter 18 on Behavior Patterns and Teams will give you an understanding the of the interpersonal dynamics of individual members that is not only enlightening and fun, but critical to sustaining a team in the long run.

A HIT is a unique, dynamic entity. It moves to its own rhythm. Chapter 19 on Phases of Team Evolution helps you understand the life stages of your team and its special requirements as it moves through them.

Long-term commitment is earned, not granted. Chapter 20 on Rewards, Recognition, and Celebration gives you ideas on how to build and sustain long-term commitment while improving the quality of work-life for team members.

All good things must come to an end. Or do they? That is the question pondered in Chapter 21 on Honorable Closure. If the answer is yes, then special attention needs to be paid to how the end is accomplished without a premature reduction in productivity and displaced team members.

Need more? Check out the general references and resources in Chapter 22.

CHAPTER EIGHTEEN

BEHAVIOR PATTERNS AND TEAMS

WHAT'S IN IT FOR YOU?

- **Learn to observe and appreciate the differences in behavior among team members**
- **Identify your own behavioral patterns**
- **Identify the behavioral patterns of others**
- **Discover why certain people click and others are like oil and water**
- **Understand how behavior patterns affect decision making, problem solving, conflict resolution, and communication on a team**
- **Create a plan for personal change to gain flexibility**

There may be nothing more fascinating and enlightening and immediately constructive for a team than the awareness and appreciation of our differences. Before we can truly understand the way others think and act (or react), we must learn to understand ourselves. That, in and of itself, can be a remarkable journey. This chapter teaches that the greatest strides occur when we apply our self-understanding in a team environment and realize that it is our very differences that make us an integral part of the whole.

I D E A

BEHAVIOR PATTERNS AND TEAMS

18.1 Patterns and Preferences

The field of psychology and the study of human behavior have shown us that human behavior repeats itself. If we are observant, we can see how we and others use a set of behaviors or patterns to function in the world. These patterns are based on preferences that each of us has for acting in certain ways in certain situations.

Taking the time to learn about and understand your own behavior patterns, as well as the behavior patterns of others, will reward you in the following ways:

- You will greatly increase your self-understanding.
- Knowledge of behavior patterns will help you know what you need and want in specific team situations.
- You will be able to change your behavior to make your team more effective.
- Your understanding of the needs and behaviors of others will improve.
- You will be better equipped to reduce personality conflicts between yourself and others.
- This knowledge may help you to help others to understand themselves.

WORKSHEET

WHAT'S IN IT FOR YOU?

- Discover whether you are a relater or a controller

BEHAVIOR PATTERNS AND TEAMS

18.2 The Relate-Control Pattern (Self-Test Part 1)

In most life circumstances, each individual must choose to be either a relater or a controller. *Relaters* are people who usually accept what the environment gives them and use it to meet their inner needs. *Controllers* are people who usually attempt to act on their environment to meet their inner needs.

Read the following descriptions of relate and control patterns and then rate yourself on the continuum by circling the appropriate number.

Relate	Control
Accommodating	Judging
Changes Behaviors Easily	Does Not Change Behaviors Easily
Risk Assessing	Risk Taking
Easygoing	Assertive
Holds Back Opinions	Gives Opinions Easily
Slow to Make Decisions	Quick to Make Decisions
Moves Away from Conflict	Moves Toward Conflict
Experience Oriented	Task/Results Oriented

4	3	2	1
Very much a relater	Somewhat a relater	Somewhat a controller	Very much a controller

W O R K S H E E T

WHAT'S IN IT FOR YOU?

• Discover whether you are an extrovert or an introvert

BEHAVIOR PATTERNS AND TEAMS

18.3 The Extroversion-Introversion Pattern (Self-Test Part 2)

As Jung* so clearly states, people have an attitude or approach to the world that is directed either outward or inward. *Extroverts* are people who outwardly express their inward thoughts and feelings through verbal and nonverbal behaviors. *Introverts*, on the other hand, are people who usually prefer not to show much of their inward thoughts to the rest of the world.

Read the following descriptions of extroverted and introverted patterns and rate yourself on the continuum by circling the appropriate number.

Extroverted   4   Very extroverted

Caring and Warm
Expressive
Animated
Talkative   3   Somewhat extroverted
Shares Feelings with Others
Feelings/Activity Oriented

Introverted   2   Somewhat introverted

Distant and Formal
Still and Calm
Unrevealing
Listener
Keeps Feelings to Self
Rational/Fact Oriented   1   Very introverted

---

*Carl Jung, *Psychological Types* (Princeton, NJ: Princeton University Press, 1971), pp. 330–339.

WORKSHEET

WHAT'S IN IT FOR YOU?

• See where you fall when the two behavioral dimensions are combined to represent an overall pattern

BEHAVIOR PATTERNS AND TEAMS

18.4 General Overall Behavior Patterns

Now that you have rated yourself on the relate-control continuum and the extroverted-introverted continuum, take the opportunity to put them together to form an overall pattern.

Circle the number you chose for the relate-control continuum in Idea 18.2. Do the same for the extroverted-introverted continuum in Idea 18.3. Now circle the title of the appropriate quadrant based on your numbers.

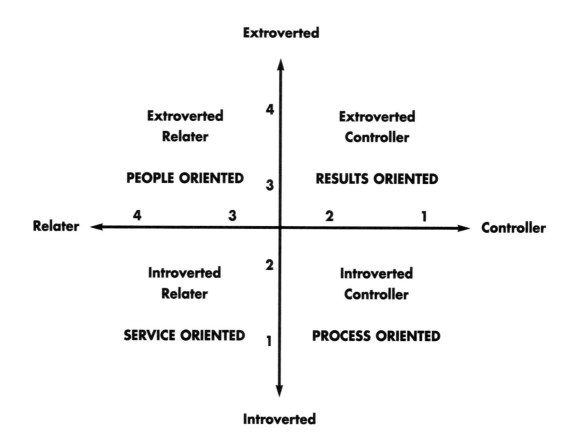

I D E A

• **Gain greater understanding of your own behavior pattern**

BEHAVIOR PATTERNS AND TEAMS

18.5 An Overview of the Behavior Patterns in Teams

A People-Oriented Person	**A Results-Oriented Person**
• Wants to like, and be liked by, others	• Wants things to happen
• Shows enthusiasm and pleasure easily	• Will tend to organize others
• Will tend to tell others of his/her feelings	• Will tend to tell others his/her ideas
• Will tend to move away from conflict	• Will compete easily when challenged
• Tends to change his/her mind quickly and easily	• Once an opinion has been formed, he/she doesn't change easily
• Is optimistic about most life experiences	• Tends to make judgments frequently
• Likes change; it is the spice of life	• Likes change, especially when he/she initiates it
• Wants and will share personal information	• Wants information quickly and in capsule form
A Service-Oriented Person	**A Process-Oriented Person**
• Wants to help or accept others	• Wants to be accurate and precise, and appreciates this in others
• Will tend to wait to hear others' ideas	• Will tend to systemize and organize the experience
• Will tend to listen carefully	• Will tend to listen for data and facts presented
• Will tend to accommodate when in conflict	• Will tend to avoid the issue, the opponent, or relevant discussion that may lead to resolution of conflict
• Will find change difficult	• Will assess experience in terms of his/her internal standards
• Tends to be quiet, calm, and slow to act	• Tends to change only when thoughtful analysis of data warrants it
• Enjoys personal consistency and consistency in others	• Judges others by their adherence to policy, process, and procedure
• Will want to hear opinions expressed by others	• Wants detailed, thorough, documented facts and data

W O R K S H E E T

WHAT'S IN IT FOR YOU?

• **Increase your understanding of the results-oriented pattern**

BEHAVIOR PATTERNS AND TEAMS

18.6 The Results-Oriented Pattern

The following in-depth characteristics are typical of the results-oriented behavior pattern. If you have determined that you have results-oriented tendencies, check the characteristics that are true for you.

- ❏ I am a fighter/competitor.
- ❏ I like to be in leadership positions.
- ❏ I will endure and "stick to my guns."
- ❏ I am quick to judge what is needed in the situation.
- ❏ If I like or don't like something, I will "tell it like it is."
- ❏ I don't hide my thoughts or ideas.
- ❏ I am decisive and strong willed.
- ❏ Sometimes I may be seen by others as pushy, domineering, or tough.
- ❏ I am a champion of change.
- ❏ I am extremely watchful for how others can screw things up.
- ❏ I want things to be done, and I don't mind doing them myself if necessary.
- ❏ I trust my approach, ideas, and instincts and if I haven't experienced it, it may not be real to me.
- ❏ I don't mind taking risks.
- ❏ I am practical and concerned with the use of ideas to create the changes I want.

If you have checked eight or more of these characteristics, you have validated that you have an affinity for this behavior pattern.

WORKSHEET

• **Increase your understanding of the people-oriented pattern**

BEHAVIOR PATTERNS AND TEAMS

18.7 The People-Oriented Pattern

The following in-depth characteristics are typical of the people-oriented pattern. If you have determined that you have people-oriented tendencies, check the characteristics that are true for you.

❑ I do not like conflict, and I will not stay if others are in conflict.

❑ I like meeting new people and getting the chance to interact with others.

❑ I am quick to adopt new fads and the latest styles.

❑ I like to accept people the way they are. What is important is people, not things.

❑ I am very sensitive to the feelings of others and feel that honesty is secondary to others' feelings.

❑ I do not hide my feelings.

❑ I am socially skilled with others.

❑ I sometimes will be seen as disorganized and late to appointments because I enjoy interacting with others.

❑ I like feeling "in on things."

❑ I am very sensitive to being rejected by others and can feel hurt.

❑ I feel it is important to be esteemed by others, and I don't mind working for that esteem.

❑ I trust what others tell me, and I take it at face value in most cases.

❑ I don't mind taking interpersonal risks with others because relationships are important.

❑ I am very enthusiastic and optimistic about people and life in general.

If you have checked eight or more of these characteristics, you have validated that you have an affinity for this behavior pattern.

WORKSHEET

WHAT'S IN IT FOR YOU?

• **Increase your understanding of the service-oriented pattern**

BEHAVIOR PATTERNS AND TEAMS

18.8 The Service-Oriented Pattern

The following in-depth characteristics are typical of the service-oriented behavior pattern. If you have determined that you have service-oriented tendencies, check the characteristics that are true for you.

❑ In a conflict situation, I will accommodate the other person's needs whenever I can.

❑ I like helping my people whenever I can.

❑ I don't mind changing my behavior if I can be helpful to others.

❑ I like to "flow with things and people" rather than judge.

❑ I don't talk too much; I prefer to listen to be helpful.

❑ I tend to be sensible and service oriented.

❑ When I make decisions, I like to confer with others to make sure they are OK with the possible outcomes.

❑ Sometimes I can get very sedentary and set in my ways because I don't like change.

❑ I like to be of service to others and enjoy harmony in the workplace.

❑ I am extremely sensitive to "change for change's sake" and want to have time to do it right.

❑ I like to get work done at a steady pace, using proven practices.

❑ I trust what people tell me and take it at face value in most cases.

❑ I think risk taking ought to be kept at a minimum by sticking to the proven ways of doing things.

❑ I think getting work done *and* helping people when you can is the best way.

If you have checked eight or more of these characteristics, you have validated that you have an affinity for this behavior pattern.

I D E A

• **Increase your understanding of the process-oriented pattern**

BEHAVIOR PATTERNS AND TEAMS

18.9 The Process-Oriented Pattern

The following in-depth characteristics are typical of the process-oriented behavior pattern. If you have determined that you have process-oriented tendencies, check the characteristics that are true for you.

❑ In conflict situations, I will avoid the issue until I've had enough; then I will fight or compete.

❑ I like to create systems and processes that make things more efficient.

❑ I have some very definite ideas that I usually won't change without logical reasons and proof.

❑ I like to weigh and judge things on the facts.

❑ When I make judgments, I will keep them to myself most of the time.

❑ I don't share my feelings with many people.

❑ I am extremely logical and data based.

❑ Sometimes I may appear to be a perfectionist with unreasonably high standards.

❑ I like continuity and proven processes that allow for accuracy in work settings.

❑ I don't like being wrong; therefore, I prepare my case in advance.

❑ I am more concerned with the hows and whys of certain work processes than how much gets done.

❑ I trust my ideas and approaches because they are usually founded on facts and data.

❑ I think that when making decisions, risk should be kept to a minimum by the analysis of all possible alternatives and consequences.

❑ I am theoretically concerned with how to make systems and processes more accurate and efficient.

If you have checked eight or more of these characteristics, you have validated that you have an affinity for this behavior pattern.

I D E A

• **Increase your understanding of how to interpret behavior patterns**

BEHAVIOR PATTERNS AND TEAMS

18.10 Important Rules to Ponder

Before you begin to delve into the behavior patterns, please remember the following guidelines:

- There is no one best pattern or preference base.
- Each pattern has its own built-in strengths and limitations, and thus, each has undeveloped potentials.
- Approximately 75 to 85% of the population will show a combination of two preferences or patterns.
- Everyone has the capacity at an instant in time to be an extrovert or introvert, controller or relater. It is the repetitive, frequent choice over time that demonstrates the pattern.
- Each of us can learn to become more appreciative of patterns different from our own.
- Each of us can learn to employ our less frequently used patterns and thus become more flexible.

I D E A

BEHAVIOR PATTERNS AND TEAMS

18.11 Overview of Other Models

Behavior patterns or styles are not a new concept. Many psychologists and writers have used various terms to describe these patterns. Although there may be slight differences among the various models, if you examine these models, you can see similarities that appear in the works of some well-known writers and researchers.*

People Oriented	**Results Oriented**
Influencer (Performax, Geier)	Dominance (Performax, Geier)
Expressive (Merrill, Wilson, Hunsaker)	Driver (Merrill, Wilson, Hunsaker)
Feeler (Jung)	Sensor (Jung)
Socializer (O'Connor, Alessandra)	Director (O'Connor, Alessandra)
Sanguine (Galen, Hypocrites)	Choleric (Galen, Hypocrites)
Service Oriented	**Process Oriented**
Steadiness (Performax, Geier)	Cautious (Performax , Geier)
Amiable (Merrill, Wilson, Hunsaker)	Analytic (Merrill, Wilson, Hunsaker)
Thinker (Jung)	Intuitor (Jung)
Relater (O'Connor, Alessandra)	Thinker (O'Connor, Alessandra)
Phlegmatic (Galen, Hypocrites)	Melancholy (Galen, Hypocrites)

*See Idea 18.29, "Bibliography," for information about other authors and models.

IDEA

WHAT'S IN IT FOR YOU?

- **Increase your ability to identify the behavior patterns of others**

BEHAVIOR PATTERNS AND TEAMS

18.12 Learning to Identify Patterns in Others

There is a basic logic to the sorting of these behavioral patterns in others. Consider using this logic tree to help you.

PERSON'S BEHAVIOR OVER TIME

Is it extroverted behavior?
- Frequent eye contact?
- Animated body movements?
- Clear facial expressions?
- Very talkative?

Is it introverted behavior?
- Infrequent eye contact?
- Sparse, slight body movements?
- Controlled facial expressions?
- Quiet, natural listener?

Is this individual results oriented? (See Idea 18.6, Results-Oriented Pattern)	Is this individual people oriented? (See Idea 18.7, People-Oriented Pattern)	Is this person service oriented? (See Idea 18.8, Service-Oriented Pattern)	Is this person process oriented? (See Idea 18.9, Process-Oriented Pattern)
As you listen to this person talk, is he/she concerned with results? Does he/she direct others? Does he/she focus on what can be accomplished?	As you listen to this person talk, is he/she very interested in others? Sensitive to others? Does he/she seem to seek the approval of others?	As you watch this person, does he/she tend to paraphrase and seek to understand? Is he/she accepting of what is said? Is he/she focused on understanding how to help?	As you watch this person, does he/she tend to question and analyze what is being said? Is he/she concerned with the accuracy of what is being said and the data that support it? Is he/she focused on reasons and asking why?
RESULTS ORIENTED	PEOPLE ORIENTED	SERVICE ORIENTED	PROCESS ORIENTED

WORKSHEET

WHAT'S IN IT FOR YOU?

- Diagnose the behavior patterns of various team members

BEHAVIOR PATTERNS AND TEAMS

18.13 Diagnosis Checklist

Using the diagram in Idea 18.12, "Learning to Identify Patterns in Others," answer the following questions. Share results with team members to see if results concur.

Team member   **Name**_____

Extroverted ❑   Introverted ❑

Results Oriented ❑   People Oriented ❑   Service Oriented ❑   Process Oriented ❑

Team member   **Name**_____

Extroverted ❑   Introverted ❑

Results Oriented ❑   People Oriented ❑   Service Oriented ❑   Process Oriented ❑

Team member   **Name**_____

Extroverted ❑   Introverted ❑

Results Oriented ❑   People Oriented ❑   Service Oriented ❑   Process Oriented ❑

Team member   **Name**_____

Extroverted ❑   Introverted ❑

Results Oriented ❑   People Oriented ❑   Service Oriented ❑   Process Oriented ❑

IDEA

• **Understand your personal decision-making preferences**

BEHAVIOR PATTERNS AND TEAMS

18.14 Behavior Patterns and Individual Decision Making

As an individual, you have a preference for the way decisions are made. Your preference could easily be at odds with the way your team makes decisions. Determine which of the personal behavior patterns and decision-making styles you most identify with in the table below. Then, on the next page, Idea 18.15, "Behavior Patterns and Group Decision Making," compare your preference with your team's decision-making guidelines.* Are they in alignment, or will you need to exercise patience and control?

	Results Oriented	**People Oriented**	**Service Oriented**	**Process Oriented**
Pace:	Fast	Fastest	Slow	Slowest
Persuaded by:	Goals/Results	Endorsement	Assurances	Data/Evidence
Means:	Decisive/Action	Spontaneous/ Reaction	Conferring/ Observing	Deliberate/ Process

Service-oriented and people-oriented team members tend to focus on people and relationships when making personal decisions. Results-oriented and process-oriented team members need to control the decision making.

---

*See Ideas 11.1–11.7, "Decision-Making Strategies."

I D E A

- **Determine if your personal preference in decision making is or is not congruent with the way your team has agreed to make decisions**

BEHAVIOR PATTERNS AND TEAMS

18.15 Behavior Patterns and Group Decision Making

Behavior preference leads to personal decision-making approaches, which may in time influence the way you prefer to make decisions when in a team. Consider your behavior pattern in light of the decision-making strategies* your team may be using. In general, if you are results oriented or process oriented, you tend to want to control the decisions.

> ☐ = Most Typical
> **WP** = Would Prefer
> **CT** = Can Tolerate
> **DP** = Does Not Prefer

	Results Oriented	**People Oriented**	**Service Oriented**	**Process Oriented**
Majority Rules	WP	WP	WP	WP
Minority Rules	CT	CT	DP	DP
Plop	DP	DP	CT	WP
Leader Decides	WP	CT	CT	CT
Consensus	DP	WP	WP	CT

*See Ideas 11.1–11.7, "Decision-Making Strategies."

IDEA

- **Understand how behavior patterns may lead to a preference for problem-solving strategies**

BEHAVIOR PATTERNS AND TEAMS

18.16 Behavior Patterns and Problem-Solving Strategies

Behavior patterns will differ greatly in the amount of tolerance and energy they may give to problem solving. Examine how each behavior pattern considers the six problem-solving steps* and see which one is descriptive of your behavior style. How might that affect your ability to deal with problem solving in your team?

☐ = Most Typical
WP = Would Prefer
CT = Can Tolerate
DP = Does Not Prefer

	Results Oriented	People Oriented	Service Oriented	Process Oriented
Problem Identification	WP	CT	CT	CT
Generate Alternatives	DP	CT	CT	CT
Examine Pros and Cons	CT	CT	CT	WP
Choose and Plan	DP	DP	WP	WP
Implement Plan	DP	DP	WP	DP
Evaluate Actions	WP	DP	DP	WP

Note: The people-oriented behavior pattern does not prefer any problem-solving strategy.

---

* See Ideas 10.1–10.17, "Problem Solving."

I D E A

- **Understand how behavior patterns may lead to a preference for conflict resolution strategies**

BEHAVIOR PATTERNS AND TEAMS

18.17 Behavior Patterns and Conflict Resolution

As you might anticipate, the way people prefer to resolve conflict* may be related to their behavior patterns. Study the chart below and see how your behavior pattern is related to the way you prefer to resolve conflict.

  ▢ = Most Typical
VFU = Very Frequent Use
SU = Some Use
DNU = Does Not Use Frequently
⟶ = Backup Prefernece

	Results Oriented	People Oriented	Service Oriented	Process Oriented
Creating	SU	SU	SU	SU
Accepting	DNU	SU	VFU	DNU
Contesting	VFU	DNU	DNU	VFU
Retreating	DNU	VFU	VFU	VFU
Modifying	VFU	VFU	SU	SU

*See Ideas 12.1–12.14, "Conflict Resolution Strategies."

IDEA

WHAT'S IN IT FOR YOU?

• **Understand how your behavior pattern may shape the way you communicate**

BEHAVIOR PATTERNS AND TEAMS

18.18 Behavior Patterns and Communication Skills

There is a very strong relationship between behavior patterns and specific communication skills.* Examine the chart below and identify your pattern's approach to communication.

VFU = Very Frequent Use
SU = Some Use
DNU = Does Not Use Frequently

	Results Oriented	**People Oriented**	**Service Oriented**	**Process Oriented**
Paraphrase	DNU	DNU	VFU	SU
Summarize	SU	SNU	VFU	SU
Ask Open-ended Questions	VFU	SU	VFU	SU
Ask Closed Questions	SU	DNU	SU	VFU
Reflect Feelings	DNU	VFU	DNU	DNU
Need Confidentiality	SU	DNU	SU	VFU

*See Ideas 13.1–13.11, "Communication."

W O R K S H E E T

WHAT'S IN IT FOR YOU?

- **Appreciate how the results-oriented person would prefer to team with others**
- **Understand your own approach to teaming**

BEHAVIOR PATTERNS AND TEAMS

18.19 The Results-Oriented Pattern and Team Behavior

Each behavior pattern has a specific approach to teaming. This approach will be both helpful and, at times, dysfunctional. Below is a short description of how the results-oriented pattern may act in a team setting. If you have a results-oriented pattern, check the boxes next to the description with which you agree.

❑ **MEETING STRUCTURE** — Would prefer as little structure as possible. Preparation may not be done. Would gravitate toward team leadership. Would grow impatient if progress or outcomes were slow in coming.

❑ **PROBLEM SOLVING** — Would be quick to define the problem; have little tolerance for the exploration of alternatives or cost-benefit analysis. Would want to decide quickly and ask others to implement.

❑ **DECISION MAKING** — Would be decisive, quick — based on his or her definition of the problem and desired outcomes. Would prefer decision-making power.

❑ **CONFLICT RESOLUTION** — Would tend to be direct and competing, attack early and often, and stick to one position. Would compromise as a last resort.

❑ **LEADERSHIP** — Would want to assume the leadership role. Would tend to test those in leadership positions.

❑ **FEEDBACK** — Would be direct in feedback to others. Would want direct feedback when receiving feedback.

❑ **COMMUNICATION** — Would tend to ask broad overview questions to understand the issues; would not tend to repeat others' points of view. Would want conversations to be to the point.

❑ **CELEBRATION** — Would not tend to "stop and smell the roses."

❑ **WHEN STRESSED** — Would tend to become domineering, harsh, impatient, and attack first. Would be sensitive to "analysis paralysis." This person will add energy and urgency to the team's deliberations.

WORKSHEET

WHAT'S IN IT FOR YOU?

- Appreciate how the people-oriented person would prefer to team with others
- Understand you own approach to teaming

BEHAVIOR PATTERNS AND TEAMS

18.20 The People-Oriented Pattern and Team Behavior

Each behavior pattern has a specific approach to teaming. This approach will be both helpful and, at times, dysfunctional. Below is a short description of how the people-oriented pattern may act in a team setting. If you have a people-oriented pattern, check the boxes next to the description with which you agree.

❑ **MEETING STRUCTURE** — Would prefer structure, but would want time to socialize and talk to people. May not do preparatory work assigned.

❑ **PROBLEM SOLVING** — An organized problem-solving process may be OK, but "lighten up" with frequent break times. The examination of "way-out" alternatives will be fun, but may adversely affect other people.

❑ **DECISION MAKING** — Would prefer to make spontaneous decisions, based on who else endorses it. Would prefer consensus that gets everyone's "buy-in."

❑ **CONFLICT RESOLUTION** — Would tend to want to compromise or modify the decision so that peace and harmony are maintained. When all else fails, the preference would be to "walk away."

❑ **LEADERSHIP** — Would prefer an egalitarian approach to leadership where everyone and anyone can be the "star of the show." Whoever is leader must be considerate of others.

❑ **FEEDBACK** — Would prefer giving and receiving feedback that is kind, helpful, and humorous.

❑ **COMMUNICATION** — Would tend to ask broad feeling questions of a personal nature. These individuals will talk easily about themselves and their feelings.

❑ **CELEBRATION** — Will enjoy a good party. Hosting celebrations would be a fine way to show off people skills and help others to enjoy life.

❑ **WHEN STRESSED** — Will tend to become impulsive and indiscriminate. Outcomes may be secondary to relationships in stressful team situations.

W O R K S H E E T

WHAT'S IN IT FOR YOU?

- **Appreciate how the service-oriented person would prefer to team with others**
- **Understand your own approach to teaming**

BEHAVIOR PATTERNS AND TERMS

18.21 The Service-Oriented Pattern and Team Behavior

Each behavior pattern has a specific approach to teaming. This approach will be both helpful and, at times, dysfunctional. Below is a short description of how the service-oriented pattern may act in a team setting. If you have a service-oriented pattern, check the boxes next to the description with which you agree.

❑ **MEETING STRUCTURE** — Likes procedures that have been proven to work. Will do the preparatory work; will want agendas and minutes to help set expectations and show progress.

❑ **PROBLEM SOLVING** — Will enjoy implementing a specific agreed-upon plan. Problem-solving techniques that allow everyone to contribute and participate will be viewed as especially helpful.

❑ **DECISION MAKING** — Will want an approach that emphasizes conferring and talking out differences. Consensus allows for everyone's "buy-in."

❑ **CONFLICT RESOLUTION** — Would tend to accept or accommodate the needs of others in a conflict situation. When giving in doesn't seem to work, the preferred strategy is to "walk away."

❑ **LEADERSHIP** — Would tend to let others exercise leadership, but would want a chance to influence the decision.

❑ **FEEDBACK** — Would tend to give and receive feedback in an indirect manner. Would want specific examples that amplify the feedback given.

❑ **COMMUNICATION** — Would tend to listen rather than talk. Tends to paraphrase a lot and would easily ask questions or reflect feelings of others. This pattern would not easily discuss self.

❑ **CELEBRATION** — Would not tend to overtly enjoy public praise. Parties or public celebrations would be privately experienced.

❑ **WHEN STRESSED** — Will tend to become sedentary and stuck in own ways. Change in present practices will be met with resistance.

W O R K S H E E T

WHAT'S IN IT FOR YOU?

- **Appreciate how the process-oriented pattern would prefer to team with others**
- **Understand your own approach to teaming**

BEHAVIOR PATTERNS AND TEAMS

18.22 The Process-Oriented Pattern and Team Behavior

Each behavior pattern has a specific approach to teaming. This approach will be both helpful and, at times, dysfunctional. Below is a short description of how the process-oriented pattern may act in a team setting. If you have a process-oriented pattern, check the boxes next to the description with which you agree.

❑ **MEETING STRUCTURE** — Would want to use all the procedures and rules needed to enhance group efficiency.

❑ **PROBLEM SOLVING** — Would want a specific problem-solving process followed. Would be especially energetic around the full exploration of all alternatives and all pros and cons.

❑ **DECISION MAKING** — Would favor an approach that resulted in the exploration of all the issues inherent in the decision. Consensus or majority rules would be seen as helpful.

❑ **CONFLICT RESOLUTION** — Would tend to avoid or retreat from direct conflict. When all else fails, would tend to compete or contest another in a team situation.

❑ **LEADERSHIP** — Would tend to want to lead by presenting expertise or showing others the evidence. Would make personal decisions by weight of data.

❑ **FEEDBACK** — Would tend to give and receive feedback in an indirect manner. Would be concerned with lack of adherence to process and norms.

❑ **COMMUNICATION** — Would tend to listen rather than talk. Would use open-ended and closed questions as well as data to get others to see his or her point of view.

❑ **CELEBRATION** — Would tend not to celebrate. To appreciate these individuals is to value their expertise and thoroughness. Discreet celebration might be accepted.

❑ **WHEN STRESSED** — Would tend to become critical of self and others. Would emphasize group procedures, norms, and accuracy to reduce the stress.

I D E A

BEHAVIOR PATTERNS AND TEAMS

18.23 Teaming with a Results-Oriented Team Member

- Be brief and get to the point.
- Ask "what" questions; avoid "why" or "how" questions.
- When in disagreement, be careful not to criticize his or her character.
- Stress the logic of your idea or approach — its practicality.
- Don't offer several alternatives. Focus on the one best idea to get results.
- If time is of concern, relate your limits to the desired "bottom line" or goal to be sought.
- When in agreement, agree with the facts, not the individual.

The results-oriented team member will need help to do the following:

- Listen and be open to other ideas, suggestions, and concerns
- Calculate risks in a more realistic manner
- Be more cautious and deliberate before deciding
- Accept the power of group collaboration
- Verbalize the reasons for his or her conclusions to others
- Understand existing sanctions or expectations.

IDEA

BEHAVIOR PATTERNS AND TEAMS

18.24 Teaming with a People-Oriented Team Member

- Stay friendly and interested in him or her as a person.
- Provide a chance for that person to verbalize his or her ideas and feelings.
- Provide opportunities for "small talk," personalizing, and being sociable.
- Provide ways to transfer his or her "talk" into actions.
- Give this individual warm, inclusive, democratic relationships.
- Provide your teammate with testimonials of others when seeking his or her acceptance.
- Provide details in writing and/or structure tasks, while remembering to limit the length or complexity of content.
- Indicate how suggested actions will benefit others.
- Focus on positive impact and consequences.

The people-oriented team member will need help to do the following:

- Become more objective in decision-making practices
- Develop more systematic, practical approaches to dealing with work tasks
- Develop more effective ways of dealing with the expectations of others
- Gain further control of his or her use of time, including commitment to prioritized goals and deadlines to accommodate such goals
- Become more firm when dealing with others by maintaining positive relationships, yet not promising what cannot be delivered.

IDEA

BEHAVIOR PATTERNS AND TEAMS

18.25 Teaming with a Service-Oriented Team Member

- Show a sincere interest in him or her as a person.
- Don't rush this person. Be patient in drawing out his or her goals.
- Be organized in presenting ideas. List specifics, steps, sequences, and where possible, outline proposals and materials.
- Ask "how" questions to elicit his or her opinions.
- Focus on procedures.
- Clearly define the roles and goals you may see this person fulfilling.
- Present new ideas or departures from the status quo with ample time to adjust to anticipated changes.
- Emphasize how his or her actions will be of service to others.

The service-oriented team member will need help to do the following:

- Initiate own ideas
- Stretch toward new challenges and untried tasks or goals
- Delegate tasks or responsibilities to others
- Appreciate his or her own accomplishments
- Say no to helping others when he or she is overloaded with work but still wants to be a loyal, conscientious group member.

IDEA

BEHAVIOR PATTERNS AND TEAMS

18.26 Teaming with a Process-Oriented Team Member

- Prepare your case in advance and have the details thought out.
- Be patient and persistent because this person is concerned with carefully developed ideas or products.
- Be precise. Support your ideas with accurate logic and information.
- If disagreeing with this teammate, be careful not to criticize his or her work efforts.
- When suggesting a change, emphasize the potential value for improved quality when implemented.
- Explain how an idea fits into the big picture or overall plan.

The process-oriented team member will need help to do the following:

- Develop a tolerance for conflict and human imperfection
- Focus on the person's worth as distinctive from his or her task competence
- Openly state and work through different perspectives
- Understand when enough data has been collected to make a decision
- Realize that feelings are as important as process when creating a high impact team
- Understand that he or she must collaborate with others.

W O R K S H E E T

• **Recognize how your pattern has strengths and weaknesses that can affect your team behavior**

BEHAVIOR PATTERNS AND TEAMS

18.27 Plan for Personal Change

Given what you have learned about behavior patterns, complete the following questions about your own pattern:

Record 3 strengths that you bring to the team.

1._____

2._____

3._____

Record 3 limitations that may adversely affect the team.

1._____

2._____

3._____

Record 3 specific behaviors you want to modify to help you be more effective on your team.

1._____

2._____

3._____

What help do you want from your teammates to assist you in making your changes?

1._____

2._____

3._____

W O R K S H E E T

WHAT'S IN IT FOR YOU?

- **Compare how compatible your behavior pattern is with other team members' behavior patterns**

BEHAVIOR PATTERNS AND TEAMS

18.28 Team Member Compatibility

Some patterns are more or less compatible with others, based on energy for certain tasks or people activities. Below is a compatibility chart for the various patterns — taking into consideration task activities or people activities. See if you can use this chart to explain some of the "chemistry" or lack of chemistry between you and someone else on your team.

RO = Results Oriented
PO = People Oriented
SO = Service Oriented
PRO = Process Oriented

X = Task Activities
O = People Activities

	EXCELLENT		GOOD		FAIR		POOR	
	1	2	3	4	5	6	7	8
RO-RO				O	X			
RO-PO			O		X			
RO-SO	X					O		
RO-PRO						X		O
PO-PO	O						X	
PO-SO	X				O			
PO-PRO		X						O
SO-SO	O	X						
SO-PRO	O	X						
PRO-PRO	X							O

I D E A

WHAT'S IN IT FOR YOU?

• **Deepen your knowledge and understanding by reading selected texts and articles**

BEHAVIOR PATTERNS AND TEAMS

18.29 Bibliography

Alessandra, T., and M. O'Connor. *The Platinum Rule.* New York: Time-Warner Books, 1996.

———. *People Smarts: Bending the Golden Rule to Give Others What They Want.* San Diego: Pfeiffer and Company, 1994.

Isachsen, O., and L.V. Berens. *Working Together: A Personality-Centered Approach to Management.* Coronado, CA: Neworld Management Press, 1988.

Jung, C.G. *Psychological Types.* Princeton, NJ: Princeton University Press, 1971.

Marston, W.M. *Emotions of Normal People.* Minneapolis, MN: Personal Press, Inc., 1979.

Merrill, D.W., and R.H. Reid. *Personal Styles and Effective Performance.* Radnor, PA: Chilton Book Company, 1981.

Myers-Briggs, I., with P.B. Myers. *Gifts Differing: Understanding Personality Type.* Palo Alto, CA: Consulting Psychologists Press, Inc., 1993.

Ornstein, R. *The Roots of the Self: Unraveling the Mystery of Who We Are.* New York: Harper Collins Publishers, 1993.

Segal, M. *Points of Influence: A Guide to Using Personality Theory at Work.* San Francisco: Jossey-Bass, Inc., 1997.

CHAPTER NINETEEN

PHASES OF TEAM EVOLUTION

WHAT'S IN IT FOR YOU?

- Enhance awareness of the five stages your team will pass through as it accomplishes its goals
- Discover strategies for pulling the team through each stage
- Have team members evaluate their perceptions of meetings that provide clues to their current phase of evolution

This chapter will describe the characteristics of the Start-Up, Downfall, Up-Lift, Outcome, and Close-Down phases that all teams experience. Checklists and worksheets will help you gauge your team members' feelings and perceptions. More importantly, you will learn what you need to provide the team to move through its current phase and progress to the next — or to sustain the Outcome phase.

I D E A

PHASES OF TEAM EVOLUTION

19.1 Five Evolutionary Phases

Teams go through five phases in the effort to achieve outcomes. How long they spend in each phase depends on the length and complexity of team goals, the number of team members, the personal style or behavior patterns of team members, and the quality of leadership and team chartering that is provided.

The Five Phases of Evolution
>Phase 1 Start-Up
>Phase 2. Downfall
>Phase 3. Up-Lift
>Phase 4. Outcome
>Phase 5. Close-Down

Why is the consideration of these phases important to a team leader?

- All teams experience the phases.
- Awareness of the phases allows the team to work through them quickly.
- Awareness prevents the team from giving up during the Downfall phase.
- Armed with knowledge, the leader can help the team focus on processes that lessen the Downfall phase.

I D E A

- **Understand the phases of team evolution in brief outline form**

PHASES OF TEAM EVOLUTION

19.2 Outline of Phases of Team Evolution

Stage	Issues	Motives	Behaviors	Needs
Start-Up	Testing and independence	To discover and develop accepted norms and guidelines	Members are polite, cautious; look to team leader for support and guidance	Orientation to purpose, outcomes, values, and "what's in it for me?"
Downfall	Conflicting expectations, internal group conflict	To express individuality, show expertise, formalize power relationships	Open hostility, tactful avoidance, lack of unity, little or no productivity or task movement	Emotional resolution, understanding of interdependence, reframing of processes, realignment of expectations
Up-Lift	Individual and group cohesion, norm clarity	To resolve conflict, achieve goal outcomes and individual acceptance	Recommitment to purpose, adherence to established process	Open exchange of information, openness and tolerance for conflict
Outcome	Functional-role interdependence, expertise	To continue performance and movement toward outcomes	Members act in appropriate roles, solutions emerge for successful task completion	Continuous improvement, constant interpersonal and performance feedback
Close-Down	Premature closure, final task completion and honorable closure	To move on to new challenges	Possible preoccupation, final feedback, recognition of team's accomplishments	Close relationships, link to future projects, honorable closure

I D E A

• Associate the phases of team evolution with other models you might have encountered

PHASES OF TEAM EVOLUTION

19.3 Overview of Other Models*

The phases of team evolution have been written about by other authors over the years. This fact will help to validate how typical it is for teams to evolve through the phases. Although there might be slight differences among the various models, if you examine them, you will see the approximate similarities that appear in the works of some writers.

	Start-Up Phase 1	Downfall Phase 2	Up-Lift Phase 3	Outcome Phase 4	Close-Down Phase 5
Ankarlo	Formation	Separation	Clarification	Unification	Maturation
Carew, Parisi-Carew, & Blanchard	Orientation	Dissatisfaction	Resolution	Production	Termination
Chang	Drive	Strive	Thrive	Arrive	Revive
Katzenback & Smith	Working Group	Pseudo-Team	Potential Team	Real Team	High Perform- ing Team
Tuckman	Forming	Storming	Norming	Performing	Mourning

*See Idea 19.20, "Bibliography," for more specific information about other authors and models. In addition, see Idea 22.1, "Team Management Reading and Resource List."

WORKSHEET

WHAT'S IN IT FOR YOU?

• **Increased understanding of Phase 1 — Start-Up**

PHASES OF TEAM EVOLUTION

19.4 Phase 1 — Start-Up

The Start-Up phase is usually filled with optimism and anticipation for most team members. The attitudes of most team members rest on their expectations of team purpose and possible organizational impact. Most people when coming to a team assignment (assuming the team membership is voluntary) want to be helpful and productive.

The Start-Up phase is full of optimism and full of team members' questions, as well. Those questions focus around issues such as the following:

- What is the team?
- What are the outcomes or deliverables?
- What are the boundaries for team actions?
- How will the team do its work?
- What interpersonal rules will the team use?
- How can the team help the organization?
- What resources does the team have?
- What does a good job look like for team performance?

There are some personal questions that team members may experience:

- What identity shall I have on the team?
- How will I connect with various team members?
- What influence will I have on this team?

W O R K S H E E T

WHAT'S IN IT FOR YOU?

• Allow team members to examine their perceptions of initial meetings in Phase 1

PHASES OF TEAM EVOLUTION

19.5 Team Member Phase 1 Checklist

In the beginning, as team members start to work together, most individuals are dealing with various questions. Those questions usually fall into two categories — organizational and personal. Distribute the following checklist to team members and ask them to circle the number on the scale that corresponds most closely to the truth of each statement for them.

Organizational

1. I am wondering what this team can become.

   No   Somewhat   Yes

   1   2   3   4   5   6   7   8   9

2. I am wondering what the team is being asked to do.

   No   Somewhat   Yes

   1   2   3   4   5   6   7   8   9

3. I am thinking this experience may ultimately be fun.

   No   Somewhat   Yes

   1   2   3   4   5   6   7   8   9

4. I am thinking that I can learn a lot from this experience.

   No   Somewhat   Yes

   1   2   3   4   5   6   7   8   9

5. I am wondering who will lead this team.

   No   Somewhat   Yes

   1   2   3   4   5   6   7   8   9

6. I am wondering if I can challenge the leader.

No   Somewhat   Yes

1   2   3   4   5   6   7   8   9

7. I am wondering how this group will make decisions.

No   Somewhat   Yes

1   2   3   4   5   6   7   8   9

8. I am wondering if I differ with a team member, how I should deal with it.

No   Somewhat   Yes

1   2   3   4   5   6   7   8   9

9. I am wondering if we can get more resources to accomplish our team outcomes.

No   Somewhat   Yes

1   2   3   4   5   6   7   8   9

10. I am wondering if the team can make a difference.

No   Somewhat   Yes

1   2   3   4   5   6   7   8   9

Personal

11. I am thinking that I don't know how I can contribute to this team.

No   Somewhat   Yes

1   2   3   4   5   6   7   8   9

12. I am wondering how to best establish my credibility with this team.

No   Somewhat   Yes

1   2   3   4   5   6   7   8   9

13. I am wondering how I can best connect interpersonally with other team members.

No				Somewhat				Yes
1	2	3	4	5	6	7	8	9

14. I am wondering how I can influence this team with my ideas.

No				Somewhat				Yes
1	2	3	4	5	6	7	8	9

15. I am wondering how other team members perceive me.

No				Somewhat				Yes
1	2	3	4	5	6	7	8	9

16. I am wondering what expectations others have for me.

No				Somewhat				Yes
1	2	3	4	5	6	7	8	9

A total of 48 points or less *per team member* may mean the team is *not* in the Start-Up phase. A total score of 49 to 96 per team member may mean the team is partially in Phase 1. A total score of 97 to 144 per team member means the group is definitely in Phase 1 — Start-Up. See Idea 196 for team leader strategies.

W O R K S H E E T

WHAT'S IN IT FOR YOU?

- **Understand what you can do as a team leader to help move your team through this phase**

PHASES OF TEAM EVOLUTION

19.6 Team Leader Phase 1 — Start-Up Strategies

Check one of the following possibilities after using the checklist in Worksheet 19.5:

- ❑ A. Average points per team member is over 97 points
- ❑ B. Average points per team member is between 48 and 97 points
- ❑ C. Average points per team member is at or under 48 points

If possibility A is chosen, consider:

- Starting the chartering process now
- Revisiting the charter with all team members (if chartering has been done)
- Having team members listen to and discuss the perceptions of team members whose scores were above 97 points
- Meeting "off-line" with team members whose scores were above 97 points
- Re-defining any and all interpersonal norms thus far established
- Having team members give and receive feedback to each other concerning team behavior. (See Worksheet 14.3, "Designated Team Feedback.")

If possibility B is chosen, consider:

- Having team members listen to and discuss the perceptions of team members whose scores were between 48 and 97 points
- Meeting "off-line" with team members whose scores were between 48 and 97 points.

If possibility C is chosen, consider:

- Moving to another checklist, possibly Phase 2 — Downfall or Phase 3 — Up-Lift, because the team is not in a start-up phase.

I D E A

PHASES OF TEAM EVOLUTION

19.7 Phase 2 — Downfall

The Downfall is characterized by team and team member disenchantment, frustration, and dissatisfaction. This state of our overall disillusionment results from what is *really* happening in team meetings in comparison to *what* team members think *ideally* should be happening. Team member expectations are not being met by other team members or by the team leader. Another reason for displeasure is that unstated, unagreed-upon expectations for interpersonal conduct have not been met.

The Downfall phase is filled with anger, frustration, initiation, worry, and conflict, yet there is a desire to strive to overcome this phase. Team members have questions such as the following:

- What is wrong with our work process?
- Why does this team member continue to act that way?
- How will this conflict be dealt with?
- What is wrong with the leadership of this team?
- Why do we keep going over the same ground?
- Why did I accept this assignment?
- Why are team members fighting/withdrawing?
- How long will this situation last?

There are also some personal questions that team members may experience:

- How shall I cope with my dissatisfaction with this team?
- How do I connect with people I do not like, but have to work with?
- How much commitment do I want to give to this team?

WORKSHEET

WHAT'S IN IT FOR YOU?

- **Allow team members to examine their perceptions of meetings in Phase 2 — Downfall**

PHASES OF TEAM EVOLUTION

19.8 Team Member Phase 2 Checklist

Circle the number on the scale for each response that best represents your perceptions of your team.

1. Are team members feeling productive?

No				Somewhat				Yes
1	2	3	4	5	6	7	8	9

2. Are there complaints about team members outside the team meetings?

No				Somewhat				Yes
1	2	3	4	5	6	7	8	9

3. Is there conflict or hostility between members?

No				Somewhat				Yes
1	2	3	4	5	6	7	8	9

4. Is there confusion about assignments among team members?

No				Somewhat				Yes
1	2	3	4	5	6	7	8	9

5. Is there apathy or general lack of interest from team members?

No				Somewhat				Yes
1	2	3	4	5	6	7	8	9

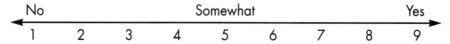

6. Is there lack of risk-taking, imagination, or initiative from team members?

No				Somewhat				Yes
1	2	3	4	5	6	7	8	9

7. Are there problems in working with other teams or individuals?

No				Somewhat				Yes
1	2	3	4	5	6	7	8	9

8. Is there lack of trust between team members?

No				Somewhat				Yes
1	2	3	4	5	6	7	8	9

9. Are decisions made that team members do not understand or agree with?

No				Somewhat				Yes
1	2	3	4	5	6	7	8	9

10. Do some members feel that their work is not recognized or rewarded by the team?

No				Somewhat				Yes
1	2	3	4	5	6	7	8	9

A total score of 30 points or less *per team member* would indicate very few symptoms of Phase 2. A total of 31 points to 60 points per member may indicate some Phase 2 Downfall symptoms. A total score of 61 points or more per team member may mean your team is in a Downfall phase. See Worksheet 19.9 for suggestions.

W O R K S H E E T

WHAT'S IN IT FOR YOU?

• Understand what you can do as a team leader to help move your team through this phase

PHASES OF TEAM EVOLUTION

19.9 Team Leader Phase 2 — Downfall Strategies

Check one of the following possibilities after using the checklist on Worksheet 19.8:

❏ A. Average points per team member is over 61 points
❏ B. Average points per team member is between 31 and 60 points
❏ C. Average points per team member is at or below 30 points

If possibility A or B is chosen, consider:

• Having the team members listen to and discuss the perceptions of team members whose scores were above 61 points
• Reviewing, recommitting to, or changing the operating guidelines established during chartering
• Reviewing, recommitting to, or changing the norms established during chartering
• Using a problem-solving process to examine and change the way the team is functioning
• Bringing in or appointing a process observer to identify the dysfunctional behaviors used by the team or team members
• Spending more meetings dealing with interpersonal issues that may have arisen among team members
• Revisiting the team purpose and outcomes to reestablish team member commitment
• Not proceeding without resolving interpersonal conflicts that may have developed.

If possibility C is chosen, consider:

• Moving to another checklist for diagnosis of another phase, because the team in not in Phase 2 — Downfall.

I D E A

PHASES OF TEAM EVOLUTION

19.10 Phase 3 — Up-Lift

The Up-Lift phase is characterized by a lessening of tension among team members and an increase in the use of processes or procedures that facilitate how work gets accomplished. The conflict resolution processes, the problem-solving processes, and the ways the group makes decisions, gives feedback, and communicates have become clearer and have received more group support. Unspoken, interpersonal issues between team members are being put to rest either by agreed-upon processes or by direct feedback. During this stage, norms are seen as important, and processes are more clearly understood.

The Up-Lift phase tends to result in team members focusing around issues such as the following:

- Can we stick to conflict resolution strategies that have worked?
- How can we help each other when conflict arises?
- How can we catch each other doing things right?
- Do we have to modify our problem solving, decision making, meeting structure, norms, etc., to help us work more effectively?
- How can we avoid conflict without producing a decision in which everyone just goes along for the sake of harmony?
- Did we allow enough time to clear away the "emotional baggage" generated in the meeting?
- How can team members show more appreciation for each other?

The following are some personal questions that team members may experience:

- Have I been fair in my approach to this team (member)?
- Can I help this team attain some sense of harmony?
- How do I show commitment in a constructive way?

W O R K S H E E T

WHAT'S IN IT FOR YOU?

• Allow team members to examine their perceptions of meetings for signs of Phase 3 — Up-Lift

PHASES OF TEAM EVOLUTION

19.11 Team Member Phase 3 Checklist

Circle the number on the scale for each response that best represents your perceptions of your team.

1. Is there an increase in team output or production?

No				Somewhat				Yes
1	2	3	4	5	6	7	8	9

2. Are the various processes such as problem solving working?

No				Somewhat				Yes
1	2	3	4	5	6	7	8	9

3. Can we change various processes used by the team to help us be more effective?

No				Somewhat				Yes
1	2	3	4	5	6	7	8	9

4. Are we avoiding conflict just for the sake of harmony?

No				Somewhat				Yes
1	2	3	4	5	6	7	8	9

5. Are people confronting each other more authentically?

No				Somewhat				Yes
1	2	3	4	5	6	7	8	9

6. Does the team spend less time on disagreements and dissension and more time on the issues that need to be discussed?

No				Somewhat				Yes
1	2	3	4	5	6	7	8	9

7. When conflict does occur, can the parties in conflict rely on others to mediate and help them work through the conflict?

No				Somewhat				Yes
1	2	3	4	5	6	7	8	9

8. Is there clarity about task assignments and follow-up?

No				Somewhat				Yes
1	2	3	4	5	6	7	8	9

9. Are team members pleased about team interactions?

No				Somewhat				Yes
1	2	3	4	5	6	7	8	9

10. Is there evidence of team members putting aside personal or expertise interests for the sake of team outcomes?

No				Somewhat				Yes
1	2	3	4	5	6	7	8	9

A total of 30 points or less *per team member* would indicate very few characteristics of Phase 3. A total of 31–60 points may indicate some presence of the Up-Lift phase. A total of 61 points or more may mean your team is in the Up-Lift phase. See Worksheet 19.12 for suggestions.

W O R K S H E E T

WHAT'S IN IT FOR YOU?

• **Understand what you can do as a team leader to help move your team through this phase**

PHASES OF TEAM EVOLUTION

19.12 Team Leader Phase 3 — Up-Lift Strategies

Check one of the following possibilities after using the checklist on Worksheet 19.11:

❑ A. Average points per team member is over 61 points
❑ B. Average points per team member is between 31 and 60 points
❑ C. Average points per team member is at or below 30 points

If possibility A or B is chosen, consider:

- Whenever possible, highlighting the successful work the team has done after the meeting
- Checking team member feelings about or impressions of team meeting(s)
- Continuing to help the team examine its processes for further refinements
- Checking with team members, when appropriate, if you think conflict has been avoided just to "keep the peace"
- Finding ways to help the team celebrate when milestones have been accomplished
- Continuing to help the team work on outcome issues.

If possibility C is chosen, consider:

- Moving to another checklist for a diagnosis of another phase, because the team in not in Phase 3 — Up-Lift.

I D E A

• **Gain a deeper understanding of Phase 4 — Outcome**

PHASES OF TEAM EVOLUTION

19.13 Phase 4 — Outcome

The Outcome phase is usually marked by team performance and deepening positive team member relationships. The team process is marked by authentic confrontative, yet collaborative, team member exchanges. Team productivity is high, and ideas are sorted and used on the basis of contribution to a common vision for team output. The team has a history of productive conflict that has built trust among team members. The team members share a common language, a set of common experiences, and a passion for a shared vision that is extraordinary. High productivity is the result.

The Outcome phase is characterized by questions and issues such as the following:

- How can the team make its outcomes more visible to the larger organizational community?
- How can team members show more appreciation for the contributions made by other team members?
- How could the work being produced be improved or reformed?
- Are there any innovative technologies on which to draw that could help the work of the team?
- How can the team sustain its superior performance?
- How can the relationships among team members be deepened?
- How does the work done by the team link to other organizational units or activities?

The following are some personal questions that team members may experience:

- Have I done some of my best work?
- Have I fully considered the ideas of others?
- Are there other ideas to be discussed?

W O R K S H E E T

WHAT'S IN IT FOR YOU?

• Allow team members to examine their perceptions of meetings for signs of Phase 4 — Outcome

PHASES OF TEAM EVOLUTION

19.14 Team Member Phase 4 Checklist

Circle the number on the scale for each response that best represents your perceptions of your team.

1. Are team members pleased with the work progress?

No				Somewhat				Yes
1	2	3	4	5	6	7	8	9

2. Are work deadlines being met?

No				Somewhat				Yes
1	2	3	4	5	6	7	8	9

3. Have strong interpersonal bonds been established between team members?

No				Somewhat				Yes
1	2	3	4	5	6	7	8	9

4. Are team members openly and respectfully confronting each other?

No				Somewhat				Yes
1	2	3	4	5	6	7	8	9

5. Is there evidence of team member collaboration and shared idea-generation?

No				Somewhat				Yes
1	2	3	4	5	6	7	8	9

6. Are linkages to the large organization becoming more vital?

No   Somewhat   Yes

1 2 3 4 5 6 7 8 9

7. Is the team exploring different technologies in order to produce better results?

No   Somewhat   Yes

1 2 3 4 5 6 7 8 9

8. Do team members show appropriate caring for each other?

No   Somewhat   Yes

1 2 3 4 5 6 7 8 9

9. Do team members demonstrate a passionate, positive attitude toward the team's outcomes?

No   Somewhat   Yes

1 2 3 4 5 6 7 8 9

10. Do team members feel part of something bigger than themselves?

No   Somewhat   Yes

1 2 3 4 5 6 7 8 9

A total of 30 points or less *per team member* would indicate very few characteristics of Phase 4. A total of 31–60 points may indicate some presence of the Up-Lift phase. A total of 61 points or more may mean your team is in the Outcome phase. See Worksheet 19.15 for suggestions.

W O R K S H E E T

WHAT'S IN IT FOR YOU?

• Understand what you can do as a team leader to help move your team through this phase

PHASES OF TEAM EVOLUTION

19.15 Team Leader Phase 4 — Outcome Strategies

Check one of the following possibilities after using the checklist on Worksheet 19.14:

❑ A. Average points per team member is over 61 points

❑ B. Average points per team member is between 31 and 60 points

❑ C. Average points per team member is at or below 30 points

If possibility A or B is chosen, consider:

- Giving as much autonomy as possible to the team by allowing all team members to take on leadership roles as appropriate
- Asking team members to represent the group's work to groups outside and inside the organization
- Asking the team to evaluate its outcome more fully
- Continually challenging the team to increase the quality of team output
- Providing the resources necessary to have the most current technology available to help the work of the team
- Helping the team celebrate its accomplishment(s)
- Helping the team anticipate the Close-Down phase by describing it and cautioning against it.

If possibility C is chosen, consider:

- Moving to a different checklist for a diagnosis of another phase, because the team in not in Phase 4 — Outcome.

I D E A

• **Gain a deeper understanding of Phase 5 — Close-Down**

PHASES OF TEAM EVOLUTION

19.16 Phase 5 — Close-Down

The Close-Down phase is mostly characterized by team member withdrawal and closure. That closure is more on a commitment level than an intellectual level, so people's energy tends to be absent as the group's work comes to an end. The team members' excitement may be conspicuously absent once the work tasks have been creatively solved. With goals closure comes an abatement of desire and focus. Honorable closure is, of course, appropriate, but the team must guard against closure that is premature.

The Close-Down phase is characterized by questions and issues such as the following:

- How can the team's work be passed off appropriately? To whom?
- Why do we have to keep meeting if the work is almost done?
- How is the team going to reach honorable closure?
- What still needs to be done before the team can formally disband?
- What sanctions can be used if a team member leaves before the work is done?
- How can the expertise of team members be used in other organizational efforts?
- What happens to individual team members when they return to everyday organizational activities?

The following are some personal questions that team members may experience:

- What's next?
- How can I maintain contact with those team members of whom I really have grown fond?
- How can I make use of the experience I have gained?

W O R K S H E E T

WHAT'S IN IT FOR YOU?

- **Allow team members to examine their perceptions of meetings for signs of Phase 5 — Close-Down**

PHASES OF TEAM EVOLUTION

19.17 Team Member Phase 5 Checklist

Circle the number on the scale for each response that best represents your perceptions of your team.

1. Has the scope of work taken on by the team been accomplished?

No				Somewhat				Yes
1	2	3	4	5	6	7	8	9

2. Is there a noticeable lack of energy in team members now that the outcomes are almost completed?

No				Somewhat				Yes
1	2	3	4	5	6	7	8	9

3. Are team members talking about other things they may move to?

No				Somewhat				Yes
1	2	3	4	5	6	7	8	9

4. Are team members feeling sad about reaching the outcomes?

No				Somewhat				Yes
1	2	3	4	5	6	7	8	9

5. Are the meetings getting shorter and shorter?

No				Somewhat				Yes
1	2	3	4	5	6	7	8	9

6. Are team members conscious of other organizational assignments they want to take?

No				Somewhat				Yes
1	2	3	4	5	6	7	8	9

7. Are team members missing meetings or delivery deadlines when this has not happened much in the past?

No				Somewhat				Yes
1	2	3	4	5	6	7	8	9

8. Are team members guarded about their emotions when that had not been the case in the most recent past?

No				Somewhat				Yes
1	2	3	4	5	6	7	8	9

9. Are people failing to process the meetings the way they used to in the past?

No				Somewhat				Yes
1	2	3	4	5	6	7	8	9

10. Are people bored and ready to move on?

No				Somewhat				Yes
1	2	3	4	5	6	7	8	9

A total of 30 points or less *per team member* would indicate very few characteristics of Phase 5. A total of 31–60 points may indicate some presence of the Close-Down phase. A total of 61 points or more may mean your team is in the Close-Down phase. See Worksheet 19.18 for suggestions.

W O R K S H E E T

WHAT'S IN IT FOR YOU?

• **Understand what you can do as a team leader to help move your team through this phase**

PHASES OF TEAM EVOLUTION

19.18 Team Leader Phase 5 — Close-Down Strategies

Check one of the following possibilities after using the checklist on Worksheet 19.17:

❑ A. Average points per team member is over 61 points
❑ B. Average points per team member is between 31 and 60 points
❑ C. Average points per team member is at or below 30 points

If possibility A or B is chosen, consider:

- Tactfully reminding team members of their commitment
- Providing a time for discussion of feelings of sadness and mourning
- Having a meeting focused on giving everyone a chance to describe what he or she may be doing next
- Giving team members a chance to declare what this experience has meant to them
- Having a celebration or formal presentation of thanks
- Making sure that assignments are fulfilled by off-line reminders and personal visits to team members.

If possibility C is chosen, consider:

- Moving to a different checklist for a diagnosis of another phase, because the team in not in Phase 5 — Close-Down.

I D E A

WHAT'S IN IT FOR YOU?

• Understand how the ideas in this book are related to each phase of team development

PHASES OF TEAM EVOLUTION

19.19 Team Phases and Book Organization

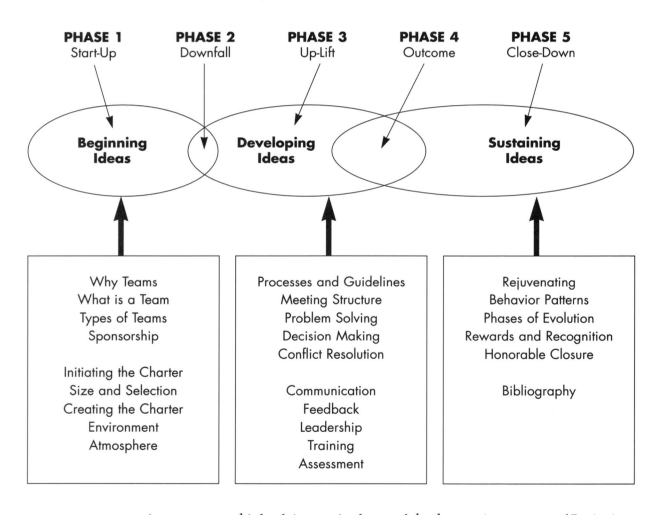

As you can see, this book is organized around the three major concepts of Beginning, Developing, and Sustaining. This diagram demonstrates how the book's different sections, chapters, and ideas are designed to aid you as a team leader in the Start-Up, Up-Lift, and Close-Down phases.

I D E A

PHASES OF TEAM EVOLUTION

19.20 Bibliography

Ankarlo, L. *Implementing Self-Directed Work Teams.* Video. Boulder, CO: Career Track Publication, 1995.

Blanchard, K.; D. Carew; and E. Parisi-Carew. *The One Minute Manager Builds High Performing Teams.* Escondido, CA: Blanchard Training and Development, Inc., 1990.

———. *Group Development and Situational Leadership II: A Model for Managing Groups.* Escondido, CA: Blanchard Training and Development, Inc., 1990.

Chang, R.Y. *Building a Dynamic Team: A Practical Guide to Maximizing Team Performance.* Irvine, CA: Richard Chang Associates, 1994.

———. *Success Through Teamwork: A Practical Guide to Interpersonal Team Dynamics.* Irvine, CA: Richard Chang Associates, 1994.

Katzenback, J.R., and D.K. Smith. *The Wisdom of Teams.* Cambridge, MA: Harvard Business School Press, 1993.

Lacoursiere, R.B. *The Life Cycle of Groups: Group Developmental Stage Theory.* New York: Human Service Press, 1980.

Tuckman, B.W. "Developmental Sequence in Small Groups," *Psychological Bulletin* 63 (1965): 384–399.

CHAPTER TWENTY

REWARDS, RECOGNITION, AND CELEBRATION

WHAT'S IN IT FOR YOU?

- **Learn the basic rules for providing effective recognition**
- **Understand the impact of intrinsic motivation**

This chapter may be short, but it's sweet. Once you understand the rules for rewarding and recognizing the team's efforts and outcomes, encourage your HIT to create its celebrations and internal recognition.

I D E A

REWARDS, RECOGNITION, AND CELEBRATION

20.1 The Power of Affirmation

Catching someone doing something right* is not done because you want someone to continue to do the right thing, although that is generally the result. You do it because it allows other people to affirm themselves. Praise, rewards, recognition, and celebration provide an opportunity to pause and reflect on the meaning of an individual's or a group's activity.

Certain types of recognition may suit a particular situation better than others:

- **Praise** is the specific public or private, verbal and nonverbal expression of appreciation for someone's actions, ideas, or activities.
- **Recognition** is a formal public announcement of privilege, title, or award based on significant action, ideas, or activities.
- **Rewards** are formal public or private gifts of money, promotions, trips, cars, stock shares, or the like based on significant actions, ideas, or activities.
- **Celebration** is a formal event at which praise, recognition, or rewards are bestowed upon individuals or groups.

Praise, recognition, rewards, and celebration are important because they

- emphasize desired behavior, not undesirable behavior
- allow others to see the implications of their own efforts
- allow others to appreciate standards of excellence
- allow the individual or team to stop and appreciate accomplishments
- bring closure to activity and effort.

Praise, recognition, rewards, and celebration may be ineffective in the following situations:

- They are not tied specifically to behavior.
- Criteria for bestowal are not clear.
- Recognition or reward is not tailored to the individual.

---

*Ken Blanchard and Spencer Johnson, *The One Minute Manager* (New York: Morrow Press, 1981) p. 39.

I D E A

- **Learn the three rules that will help guarantee that recognition given will be received with the proper intent**

REWARDS, RECOGNITION, AND CELEBRATION

20.2 Rules for Effective Recognition and Reward

In order for praise, recognition, or rewards to be effective, consider the following rules:

- **It must be *immediate*, not delayed.** The further away from the behavior, action, or activity the praise, recognition, or reward is, the less it serves as a pleasure stimulus for the receiver.

- **It must be *personal*, not organizational.** When recognition, reward, or praise is given to all, across-the-board, it mutes the special nature of an individual's actions. Therefore, raises given to everyone at the end of the year soon become entitlement, not a sign of outstanding achievement.

- **It must be *certain*, not random.** Recognition, reward, or praise that is capriciously dependent upon the frame of mind of the giver will at best be viewed as benevolence. People in organizational settings must believe that there is a **sure** connection between their effort and actions and the payoff.

IDEA

REWARDS, RECOGNITION, AND CELEBRATION

20.3 Extrinsic and Intrinsic Motivation

People do extraordinary things for various reasons. While extrinsic motivators such as praise, rewards, and recognition from others may have become the primary motivator for some, consider the following ideas:

- People who are motivated by extrinsic reinforcers stop doing desired behaviors when the external reinforcers are discontinued.
- People who are motivated by extrinsic reinforcers often lose touch with themselves and act out of compliance or defiance.
- There are three basic internal motivators for most people:
  1. A desire for a positive interpersonal relationship
  2. A desire to grow
  3. A desire to give to something bigger than themselves.
- Recognition or rewards that do not allow an individual to acknowledge and respond to one of these internal motivators may ultimately keep the individual environmentally dependent.

These ideas imply that the meaning of the work that the team does may be the biggest intrinsic motivator. To be part of something truly unique, outrageously excellent, and/or shared with others may be so emotionally addictive that it is its own reward. Perhaps then, a leader who can get team members in touch with the value of the team and create an atmosphere of excellence will be giving team members their greatest reward.

W O R K S H E E T

WHAT'S IN IT FOR YOU?

• **Evaluate and discuss how the team celebrates its activities**

ASSESSING TEAM PROCESS

20.4 Celebration Evaluation Checklist

Circle the number that best represents your perceptions of how the team celebrates its activities.*

1. Do team members celebrate the team's small accomplishments?

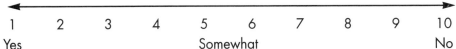

1	2	3	4	5	6	7	8	9	10
Yes				Somewhat					No

Behavior used to judge: _____

_____

2. Do team members directly and specifically praise one another?

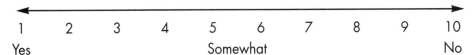

1	2	3	4	5	6	7	8	9	10
Yes				Somewhat					No

Behavior used to judge: _____

_____

3. Do team members give each other credit for helpful ideas?

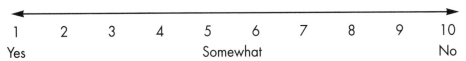

1	2	3	4	5	6	7	8	9	10
Yes				Somewhat					No

Behavior used to judge: _____

_____

4. When talking to groups outside the team, do team members represent the team output as a total team effort?

1	2	3	4	5	6	7	8	9	10
Yes				Somewhat					No

Behavior used to judge: _____

_____

5. Do individual team members publicly give credit to others on the team?

1	2	3	4	5	6	7	8	9	10
Yes				Somewhat					No

Behavior used to judge: _____

_____

6. Does the team do enough celebration of its accomplishments?

1	2	3	4	5	6	7	8	9	10
Yes				Somewhat					No

Behavior used to judge: _____

_____

7. Has the team brainstormed fun things to do to celebrate team accomplishments?

1	2	3	4	5	6	7	8	9	10
Yes				Somewhat					No

Behavior used to judge: _____

_____

8. Are you satisfied with the way the team celebrates its accomplishments?

1	2	3	4	5	6	7	8	9	10
Yes				Somewhat					No

Behavior used to judge: _____

_____

*See Ideas 20.1–20.4, "Rewards, Recognition, and Celebration," for elaboration.

CHAPTER TWENTY ONE

HONORABLE CLOSURE

WHAT'S IN IT FOR YOU?

• Recognize when the team has run its course
• Honor the team by understanding the need and process of closure

If all good things must come to an end, then too, all things should come to a good end. Providing honorable closure allows team members to look back with pride and forward with anticipation.

I D E A

• **Understand why honorable closure to a team or a phase of a team's life is an important consideration**

HONORABLE CLOSURE

21.1 All Good Things Must Come to an End

Depending upon the type of team you have in place, the work of the team will come to an end. In the case of a task force or temporary committee that completes its work, you should bring the team's activities to an honorable end.

Why is honorable closure important?

- Closure will give those who worked on the team a chance to be acknowledged.
- It will give the rest of the organizational community a chance to acknowledge the team's work.
- It will let the organization know that teamwork is valued.
- It will give an opportunity to publicize the team's output.
- Thought must be given to how to maintain performance momentum, if appropriate.
- If the work or team has been secret and must remain so, create closure that is not public, but allows individuals within the team to honor one another and acknowledge that they and their work existed.
- As Bennis and Biederman* note, because the intense energy generated in great teams cannot be sustained indefinitely, after the team produces, it usually will end.
- Many teams naturally wane because a paradigm may shift, pessimism may set in, moral issues may arise, and what the group initially set out to do has been accomplished.
- When high performing teams end, the "post partum depression is often so fierce and the intensity of collaboration a potent drug, that it may make everything else, after that, drab and ordinary" (Bennis and Biederman, 1997).

---

*Warren Bennis and Patricia Ward Biederman, *Organizing Genius: The Secrets of Creative Collaboration* (Reading, MA: Addison-Wesley Publishing Company, 1997), p. 29.

I D E A

HONORABLE CLOSURE

21.2 How to Honor the End of a HIT

1. Publicize the team's outcomes in the organization's annual report.
2. Hang a photograph of the team, with team names and achievements, in the main entrance of the organization's facility for visitors to view.
3. Use members of a successful team as consultants to other teams.
4. Create stories of the team's success to illustrate a vision for other ongoing teams.
5. Use members of a successful team to help select prospective team members for future teams.
6. Honor the work of the team by implementing the recommendation produced by the team.
7. When complimenting the team's output to others, explain why the outcomes were so valuable to the organization's progress.
8. Give those who served on the successful team a brief rest without work obligation, if possible and desired.
9. Thank the families of successful teams for the sacrifices that were made on behalf of the team members.
10. Give the team members a one-time monetary gift or reward for the team's performance.

I D E A

WHAT'S IN IT FOR YOU?

- Discover ways to keep performance momentum going after the primary team no longer exists or original team members are no longer involved

HONORABLE CLOSURE

21.3 And the HITs Keep Coming

If you, as a sponsor or team leader, are concerned with how the work of the team will be continued, you should take steps to ensure it will happen. To continue the performance momentum, consider the following ideas:

- Ask the team to suggest how the momentum could be fostered.
- Ask selected team members to head up various efforts or pilot programs that continue the team's work.
- Ask team members to suggest who might be the best people to pick up where they left off.
- In the meetings before the team closes, ask the team to include those people who must implement the team's recommendations in order to ensure a smooth transition.
- Ask the team what vested interests may create barriers to the continued momentum of its work.

W O R K S H E E T

• **Conduct an exercise with team members to bring honorable closure to their experience**

HONORABLE CLOSURE

21.4 Honorable Closure Worksheet

A helpful way to create honorable closure with team members is to ask them to think about and share their experience on the team. Ask them to use the following questions to structure their thinking. This exercise can be effective at the end of any particularly demanding project or phase of the team's life.

Thankfulness:
For what do you feel thankful as you reflect on your team experience?

_____

_____

_____

Learning:
What are two or three of the greatest lessons for you as you reflect on your team experience? _____

_____

_____

Challenge:
What stretched you or challenged you the most as you reflect on your team experience? _____

_____

_____

Forgiveness:
Is there anything that needs to be forgiven or "made right" before you move on?

_____

_____

_____

CHAPTER TWENTY TWO

BIBLIOGRAPHY

WHAT'S IN IT FOR YOU?

• **Learn more about the nature and nurturing of teams from some of the latest research and literature available**

22.1 Team Management Reading and Resource List

This resource list recommends some of the most cogent and insightful writing on team work. For references on specific team-related issues, see the following: Idea 10.19, "Problem Solving," Idea 12.14, "Conflict Resolution," Idea 18.29, "Patterns of Behavior," and Idea 19.20, "Phases of Team Development."

Bennis, Warren, and Patricia Ward Biederman. *Organizing Genius: The Secrets of Creative Collaboration*. Reading, MA: Addison-Wesley Publishing Company, 1997.

Bluestone, Barry, and Irving Bluestone. *Negotiating the Future: A Labor Perspective on American Business*. New York: Basic Books, 1990.

Bucholz, Steve, and Thomas Roch. *Creating the High Performance Teams*. New York: John Wiley and Sons, 1987.

Bunker, B.B., and B.T. Alban. *Large Group Interventions: Engaging the Whole System for Rapid Change*. San Francisco: Jossey-Bass, Inc., 1996.

Crensencio, T. *The Tao of Teams: A Guide to Team Success*. San Diego: Pfeiffer and Company, 1994.

Grodan, Jack. "Work Teams: How Far Have They Come?" *Training* (October 1992): 59–65.

Hackman, J.R., ed. *Groups That Work (and Those That Don't)*. San Francisco: Jossey-Bass, Inc., 1993.

Harrington-Mackin, D. *Keeping the Team Going: A Tool Kit to Renew + Refuel Your Workplace Teams*. New York: American Management Association, 1996.

Hayes, Nick. *Successful Team Management*. London: International Thompson Business Press, 1997.

Katzenback, Jon R., and Douglas K. Smith. *The Wisdom of Teams: Creating the High-Performance Organization*. New York: Harper Business, 1993.

Larson, C.E., and F.M. LaFasto. *Team Work: What Must Go Right/What Can Go Wrong.* Newbury Park, CA: Sage Publications, 1989.

Lawler, Edward E., III. *The Ultimate Advantage: Creating the High Involvement Organization.* San Francisco: Jossey-Bass, Inc., 1992.

Manz, Charles C., and Henry Sims, Jr. "Leading Workers to Lead Themselves: The External Leadership of Self Managing Work Teams," *Administrative Senior Quarterly* 32 (1987): 106–128.

Margension, Charles, and Dick McCann. *Team Management.* London: Mercury Books, 1990.

Melagan, Patricia, and Christo Nel. *The Age of Participation: New Governance for the Workplace and the World.* San Francisco: Berrett-Koehler Publishing, 1995.

Mohrman, S.A., and S.G. Cohen. *Designing Team-Based Organizations.* San Francisco: Jossey-Bass, Inc., 1994.

Nirember, John. *Leading Teams.* Homewood, IL: Business One Irwin; San Diego: Pfeiffer and Company, 1993.

Osburn, Jack; Linda Moran; Ed Musselwhite; and John Zenger. *Self-Directed Work Teams.* Homewood, IL: Business One Irwin, 1990.

Parker, G.M. *Cross Functional Teams.* San Francisco: Jossey-Bass, Inc., 1992.

———. *Team Players and Teamwork.* San Francisco: Jossey-Bass, Inc., 1990.

Riley, Pat. *The Winner Within: A Life Plan for Team Players.* New York: Berkeley Publishing Group, 1993.

Schwarz, R.M. *The Skilled Facilitator: Practical Wisdom for Developing Effective Groups.* San Francisco: Jossey-Bass, Inc., 1994.

Shaw, M.E. *Group Dynamics: The Psychology of Small Group Behavior.* New York: McGraw-Hill, 1981.

Steckler, Nicole, and Nanette Fandos. "Building Team Leader Effectiveness," *Organizational Dynamics* (Winter 1995): 20–35.

Wellins, R.S.; W.C. Byham; and G.R. Dixon. *Inside Teams: How 20 World Class Organizations Are Winning Through Teamwork.* San Francisco: Jossey-Bass, Inc., 1994.

Wellins, R.S.; W.C. Byham; and J.M. Wilson. *Empowered Teams.* San Francisco: Jossey-Bass, Inc., 1991.

Zander, A. *Making Groups Effective.* San Francisco: Jossey-Bass, Inc., 1989.